Foreign at Home
and Away

To Lisa —
with best wishes
Margaret Bender
2002

Foreign at Home and Away

Foreign-Born Wives in the U.S. Foreign Service

Margaret Bender

An ADST-DACOR Diplomats and Diplomacy Series Book

Writers Club Press
San Jose   New York   Lincoln   Shanghai

Foreign at Home and Away
Foreign-Born Wives in the U.S. Foreign Service

Writers Club Press
an imprint of iUniverse, Inc.

For information address:
iUniverse, Inc.
5220 S. 16th St., Suite 200
Lincoln, NE 68512
www.iuniverse.com

ISBN: 0-595-22521-7

Printed in the United States of America

For John, Heather, and Alexandra,

and for my mother, Lorna, who opened the door and kept it open

Contents

Foreword

The ADST-DACOR Diplomats
and Diplomacy Series

Margaret Bender's perceptive *Foreign at Home and Away* is the first ADST-DACOR Diplomats and Diplomacy Book that examines the roles played by Foreign Service spouses and the particular circumstances of those who are foreign-born wives.

The Association for Diplomatic Studies and Training (ADST), a non-profit educational organization founded in 1986, complements the work of the Foreign Service Institute and, together with Diplomatic and Consular Officers, Retired (DACOR), aims to support and enhance the effectiveness of U.S. diplomacy through education. In 1995, ADST and DACOR created the Diplomats and Diplomacy Series to increase public knowledge of and appreciation for the involvement of American diplomats in world history. Books published in this series seek to demystify diplomacy by telling the story of those who have conducted our foreign relations.

Often overlooked in this story is the important part played by diplomats' families. While Foreign Service officers are interacting primarily on a professional level in host countries, their spouses and children are meeting local citizens in homes, offices, schools, markets, places of worship, clubs, and volunteer organizations. Together, the diplomats and their families present to the world's people a firsthand, personal image of the United States.

Increasingly, that image reflects the multicultural nature of American society, as U.S. foreign affairs agencies actively recruit Americans with differing cultural backgrounds to reflect American society more accurately and to take advantage of their language skills and cross-cultural knowledge. Meanwhile, the United States has, for many years, displayed a multicultural face to the world through the foreign-born spouses of many of its diplomats.

In *Foreign at Home and Away*, Australian-born writer Margaret Bender has drawn on her own twenty-five years' experience as a Foreign Service wife to describe diplomatic life from the perspective of foreign-born wives, estimated to be one-third to one-half of the women married to U.S. Foreign Service officers. From in-depth interviews with forty women from twenty-eight countries, she has gathered stories of their backgrounds, of the challenges they face, and of the contributions they make to the representation of the United States abroad. Their stories are woven throughout the book as they relate to such topics as cultural transitions, work, children, the special issues of senior wives and CIA wives, marital problems, life after the Foreign Service, and the experience of returning to their home countries after long absences.

Foreign at Home and Away adds a missing but essential chapter to the story of the U.S. Foreign Service. Its relevance extends to men and women in similar situations—most notably, in the military, international organizations, and transnational business—and will appeal to all readers drawn to authentic, well-told, personal stories.

Kenneth L. Brown, President
Association for Diplomatic Studies
   and Training
Arlington, Virginia
www.adst.org

Alan W. Lukens, President
Diplomatic and Consular
   Officers Retired
Washington, D.C.
www.dacorbacon.org

Acknowledgments

To be told a story is to receive a gift, and I am extremely grateful to the women who generously shared their stories with me. Without their willingness to relate their experiences candidly and to express their feelings openly, this book would not have been possible.

I would also like to thank Margery Thompson, publishing coordinator at ADST, for her advice and encouragement; the director and staff at FLO; and the AAFSW president, board members, and office manager. Thanks also to Billie Ann Lopez, Diane Castrodale, Howard Kavaler, and the many friends who, at tactful intervals over the four years of the project, gently enquired, "How is it going?"

Most of all, thanks to my husband, John, and my daughters, Heather and Alexandra, for their continuous support for all my endeavors.

Note to the Reader

Today, both men and women are employed by the foreign affairs agencies of the government of the United States. Many male American-born foreign service officers (FSOs) have American-born wives; many female American-born foreign service officers have American-born husbands (and some have foreign-born husbands). However, the focus of this book is on the foreign-born women married to American-born male foreign service officers.

Strictly speaking, foreign service officers are men and women who have passed the foreign service exam set by the Department of State. For the purposes of this book, I use the term foreign service officer in a broader sense to include those individuals who are professional and support employees of other agencies now represented in American embassies. While the agency affiliations and responsibilities of the employees may differ, the experiences of their families are similar. The women in this book are, or were, married to employees of the Department of State (USDS), United States Agency for International Development (USAID or AID), United States Information Service/Agency (USIS or USIA),[1] Foreign Commercial Service (FCS), Foreign Agricultural Service (FAS), and the Central Intelligence Agency (CIA).

Prologue

The gravestone in Arlington National Cemetery is small, the uniform size for stones marking the thousands of graves in this most sacred of American ground. As on the other markers covering the grassy slopes—most of which record military affiliation, war service, and state of residence—the information engraved in its surface is sparse. This one reads: "Prabhi G. Kavaler, December 3, 1952–August 7, 1998, Department of State, Foreign Service Officer." Like the inscriptions on all of the surrounding markers, there is so much that it doesn't say.

It doesn't tell you that Prabhi was killed by a terrorist bomb while she worked at her desk in the American embassy in Nairobi, Kenya, one of twelve Americans and over two hundred Kenyans who died in the explosion. It doesn't tell you how beautiful she was, or that she loved Shakespeare, used to ride a motorcycle, enjoyed giving dinner parties, valued her friends. It doesn't tell you about Howard and Tara and Maya, the husband and small daughters she left behind. It also doesn't tell you that the United States was her adopted country. Prabhi was an American by marriage and naturalization.

She was born Prabhi Guptara in Amritsar, India, near the border with Pakistan. Her parents came from Lahore in Pakistan: her father, an Oxford-educated English teacher; her mother, a nurse. They were of different religions—he, a Hindu, and she, a Christian—so at Partition in 1947 they moved from predominantly Muslim Pakistan to Amritsar. When Prabhi was four years old, her father died and her mother moved Prabhi and her two older brothers to New Delhi.

Prabhi attended parochial schools. She earned her bachelor and master of arts degrees at the Delhi School of Economics, majoring in sociology, and a doctorate, also at the Delhi School of Economics, writing her thesis on the history of the Indian cinema industry. She went to work for Voice of America as a stringer, writing and broadcasting, and then joined the North India Branch of the United States Information Agency (USIA). In 1979, her American supervisor at USIA introduced her to one of his colleagues, Howard Kavaler, a lawyer and first-tour consular officer. Howard was independent and outspoken, just like Prabhi.

They courted for about two and a half years, until Howard was transferred to Jerusalem. Prabhi remained in New Delhi. Howard returned and proposed, and they were married in July of 1982 in England, where Prabhi's mother and a brother were living at the time. There is no civil marriage in Israel (Howard is Jewish and Prabhi was not) so it was easier for them to be married in England. After the wedding, they returned to Jerusalem. Six months later, while on leave in the United States, Prabhi was naturalized. With American citizenship, she became eligible to apply for the part-time jobs in the embassy that are available to foreign service family members posted overseas.

In 1984, Howard was transferred to Islamabad, Pakistan, where he was the narcotics control officer, and Prabhi found a job as the systems manager in the embassy. The Islamabad assignment was curtailed the following year when Howard was directed back to Jerusalem to take over as head of the Consular Section. Prabhi again found work in the General Services Office (GSO), and in 1987 she took the examination for the Specialist Program for Administrative Officers. As part of this program, she spent a year in Washington while Howard stayed in Jerusalem. They visited in one or the other place every three months.

That year, 1988, their first daughter, Tara, was born at Columbia Hospital for Women in Washington, D.C., and Prabhi sat for and passed the foreign service exam. Her status changed from that of a specialist to a generalist. She was now a foreign service officer. She and Howard secured a tandem assignment to the Philippines and served there in Manila until 1990, when they were transferred to Nairobi. Howard's job on the first Nairobi tour was labor attaché. Prabhi was supposed to do her first consular tour, but because no consular position was available, the Department allowed her to take the assistant administrative officer position.

They returned to Washington in 1992, bought a house in McLean, a northern-Virginia suburb, and entered French language classes in preparation for assignments to Paris. Their second daughter, Maya, was born in 1993, at Sibley Hospital in Washington, just before the family's departure for France. Howard was deputy consul-general concentrating on American services, and Prabhi did her consular tour working the visa line. They stayed two years in Paris and returned to Washington in 1995, moving back into their house in McLean. Prabhi spent a year working in the personnel department and a year on the Mexico desk. Then came the opportunity to go back to Nairobi.

Howard was appointed the U.S. representative to the United Nations environment program. The only job available for Prabhi was the same one she had held on their previous tour eight years earlier, but she accepted it so they could go together. In July of 1998 they packed up once more and left for their second tour in Nairobi.

They arrived in the third week in July and moved into temporary quarters. One car had arrived, plus the airfreight, which remained unopened pending their move to their permanent house. The day before the bombing, Prabhi was sick and stayed home. It was the summer transfer season and one of her jobs was to get shipments cleared through customs. Her position had been vacant for six months and the staff was hard-pressed. So the next morning, August 7, although she still didn't feel well, she went to work.

About 10:15 a.m., Howard stopped by her office, which was on the first floor of the embassy. They chatted for a while and she asked him to visit the Community Liaison Office (CLO) to find out about the school bus schedule for Tara and Maya. Howard left Prabhi's office, made a brief stop at his own office, which was on the second floor on the other side of the building, and then headed to the CLO's office. A few seconds later, he heard a loud thud on the ceiling. Then the building collapsed.

He picked his way down a stairwell, which was filled with rubble, and reached the outside. He looked around for Prabhi, certain that if he had managed to get out, she would have too. At the side of the building where her office was located, he saw the remains of the truck that had contained the bomb. It was on fire and billowing smoke. The embassy building was a wreck, and Prabhi was nowhere in sight. Other officers who had escaped were preventing people from returning to the building, but Howard persuaded them to let him go back to look for Prabhi. He made his way to her section, where he saw the bodies of some of the Kenyan employees, but there was only debris where Prabhi's office had been: concrete, wires, pieces of furniture. He couldn't find her. Her body was found later by another searcher.

Together with the families of the other Americans killed in the blast, Howard, Tara, and Maya flew back to the United States. Dazed and grieving, the families were met at Andrews Air Force Base by the president and other government officials and colleagues. The flag-draped coffins were unloaded from the airplane and lined up in the hangar. The foreign service was in mourning.

The tenants in the family's McLean house found another place to live as quickly as they could, and Howard and the girls moved back home. Friends and neighbors who had happily waved them off just weeks before gathered in shock and grief. Prabhi was buried at Arlington on August 18, her coffin lowered into the grave by a military honor guard. Clearly visible over the trees and across the Potomac were the upper floors of the State Department. The officiating clergyman tried to comfort those of us who were present by asking us to remember that, while Prabhi's death was tragic, she had died in the service of the country she loved, one that she had chosen as her own.

"She was proud to be an American, and very mindful of the opportunities she had," Howard said. "She didn't take things for granted, as we who are born here often do. She wasn't necessarily concerned with advancing her career: the girls were always the most important priority. She was able to strike a nice balance, striving to do her best at work while being concerned for the girls and me. She also had a love of learning. Her upbringing had not been an affluent one, but she always felt that because she had a good education, she could take care of herself."

Howard has established a perpetual scholarship fund through the American Foreign Service Association (AFSA) in Prabhi's name. Each year the fund grants $1,000 to a foreign service dependent. When setting up the scholarship, Howard was asked if he wanted to limit it to women or children who were Asian or part-Asian. He said no, that Prabhi would not have wanted that. She was proud of her Indian background, but she believed that having made the decision to become an American, and especially to represent the country, she would be giving the wrong signals to hold herself out as an Indian. The only stipulation for the scholarship would be that it go to a good student who was in need of the money.

A few miles away from the cemetery, there is another memorial to Prabhi in the community she called home. Four young cherry trees have been planted outside the Dolley Madison Library in McLean. Prabhi often took the girls to this library and to the community center across the street. The inscription on the plaque in front of the trees reads: "In memory of Prabhi G. Kavaler, Foreign Service Officer, wife of Howard Kavaler, mother of Tara and Maya Kavaler, and resident of McLean, killed August 7, 1998, in the bombing of the United States Embassy in Nairobi, Kenya." The information is still incomplete, but maybe in the years to come, when the cherry trees are tall, visitors to the library will ask about her and the librarian will direct them to this book, where they will read not just about her death, but about her life, and the lives of other women who were born in other countries and through their marriages became part of the American foreign service.

Introduction

Driving home from Prabhi's burial, I kept thinking about her mother grieving by the graveside. I wondered how many other mothers like her could have been burying their daughters that day, so far away from the countries in which they had raised them. I had noticed a few other foreign-born wives among the mourners at the cemetery; some I knew well, others just by sight. At home, I took a pencil and paper and listed all the foreign-born foreign service wives I knew. In a few minutes I had twenty names, with my own at the top. I thought: If I know this many, there must be lots more.

I paid a visit to the Family Liaison Office (FLO) at the Department of State, the office responsible for employee family issues, and asked them for some figures. How many foreign-born wives are there in the foreign service? They didn't know; there are no statistics. A similar request of the Central Intelligence Agency brought the same answer: no data. From somewhere, FLO came up with the arbitrary number they use when asked: one-third of all the wives of foreign service officers are believed to be foreign-born.

Anecdotal evidence suggests that the number is higher. For example, friends taking an informal count for me in 2000 reported that at the American embassy in Seoul, South Korea, out of 93 wives, 50 were foreign-born, and at the embassy in Tashkent, Uzbekistan, in the same year, at least half of all the wives were foreign-born. I have since heard of similar percentages found in other embassies over the years.

That there are so many should probably come as no surprise, considering the fact that single men will socialize with the women in the communities in which they find themselves. In the foreign service, those communities are in other countries. Also, many American foreign service officers are former Peace Corps volunteers, and some of them have already married foreign women during their Peace Corps days overseas.

My own foreign-born status is not something I have dwelt on over the twenty-five years I have spent as a foreign service wife, and I had never really discussed the subject with the other foreign-born wives I knew. I was born and raised in Australia and have served with my husband in India, Germany, Israel, Sri Lanka, Austria, and South Korea. I had read books about foreign service life in general, and others about raising children overseas, but I had never seen anything written about the foreign-born women. I started to wonder about how others' experiences compared with mine and I decided to gather some of their stories. Where did they come from? How did they meet their husbands? How did they feel about representing a country that was not, at least in the beginning, their own? And, what about their children?

I advertised my project in various in-house and expatriate newsletters, but received only three responses. So I began to approach the women I knew personally and contacted others who were referred to me through intermediaries. It became clear early on that a personal introduction was crucial to an agreement to be interviewed. All together, I spoke with thirty-two women at length, received five written contributions from women not available for a personal interview, and referred to three oral histories already on file with the Oral History Project of the Associates of the American Foreign Service Worldwide (AAFSW). (Formerly known as the Association of American Foreign Service Women, this is an independent organization devoted to the well-being of families in the foreign service.) I supplemented two of the oral histories with personal interviews of the subjects.

I designed a questionnaire and used it to start conversations, which invariably took directions that were important to the women themselves. Instead of structuring the book as a string of individual oral histories, I decided to divide it into chapters devoted to the main topics of common interest. The women's backgrounds are important to the story, however, so

I have placed this information in a separate section at the back of the book. Readers can refer to this section as they wish. It seemed less disruptive to the narrative to do it this way rather than to tell each woman's story in the middle of a discussion. I have, however, inserted five longer background stories in different places throughout the book.

I have not quoted from all the interviews, and only those women who are quoted by name appear in the background section. For easier readability, conversations have been edited and condensed, but the women's observations and opinions remain their own. Except for Faye Barnes, Maria Bauer, Lesley Dorman, Elisabeth Herz (whose story is told in installments throughout the book), the women are identified by first name only. Some names have been changed or omitted altogether for reasons of security or privacy.

The women range in age from thirties to eighties and come from Australia, Austria, Belgium, Canada, Chile, Colombia, Croatia, Czech Republic, Denmark, Fiji, France, Gabon, Germany, Guatemala, India, Indonesia, Italy, Japan, Kuwait, Lebanon, Mexico, New Zealand, Peru, Poland, South Korea, Taiwan, Trinidad and Tobago, Turkey, and the United Kingdom. The majority married in their mid-twenties or early thirties; most of them had two children (some had none and some had one, but none had more than two); and all but two of the women were first wives (to answer the question of an American-born woman who was sure a foreign wife must have been an exotic temptation to an already-married man).

A few of the couples met in the United States and some met in third countries, but most of them met in the woman's home country. Seven couples were already married before the husband joined the foreign service, including the two couples in which both husband and wife were foreign-born. The majority of the women had never visited the United States before marriage. Others had come for short vacations, longer periods for schooling, or in a few cases, extended periods for work.

Many parents traveled long distances to attend their son's wedding, while others met their new daughter-in-law in the United States after the marriage had already taken place abroad. One woman reported disapproval from her husband's family and three women described strong opposition to their marriages from their own families. The majority, however, spoke warmly of the open manner in which they were welcomed into their husbands' families and of their subsequent relationships with them.

These women experience immigrant life in a unique way. While most expressed pride in the United States and their role in its foreign service, they said that when they are posted overseas, they are foreign, and when they come back to the United States, they are still foreign.

Chapter One

Foreign Service Wife

Elisabeth Kremenak had to get through two interviews before leaving Vienna in 1957 to be married, and she dreaded both of them. One was with her father, and the other was with Professor Antoine, the chairman of the Department of Obstetrics and Gynecology at Vienna's University Clinic, where she was finishing her four years of residency. Elisabeth had decided to be a physician when she was eight years old and had persevered in spite of opposition from her father and from the professor, who disapproved of women in medicine and included only two in his department.

Just days before her departure for Bangkok, Thailand, where the wedding was to take place, Elisabeth sat with her father at home, where she still lived, drinking coffee after dinner. She knew he was planning to go out, and she had timed the conversation to take place just before he was to leave.

"Well, Father, I am going to get married," she began.

"Married! To whom? Another physician?"

"No, Father. He's a diplomat."

"A diplomat—a gypsy!"

"Yes, Father."

"Well, where is he?"

"He is at present posted in Phnom Penh in Cambodia."

"Austria doesn't have a representative in Cambodia."

"Well, he's not Austrian, Father—he's American."

It was the first time she had ever seen her father speechless. He got up from his chair and left the room.

She had met with Professor Antoine in his office. He was a world-renowned, brilliant physician and, like most of his students, Elisabeth loved and admired him. She often assisted him with his operations. Plans had already been made for her also to study psychiatry so that she could pursue her dream of combining it with her ob/gyn training to treat psychosomatic illnesses in women. When she went to see him, he began discussing a research project that would take her a year to complete.

"Professor Antoine, I'm leaving."

"Leaving? Why? Are you going to another hospital?"

"No, Professor. I'm getting married."

His only reply was a very quiet "Thank you," and she was dismissed—miserable.

The following day, she was to assist him in a cancer surgery. She scrubbed up and took her place at the operating table. He said, "No, you operate. I will assist you." After the operation was over, he quizzed her about its outcome. She replied that she thought she had got everything out and asked his opinion. He became uncharacteristically emotional, saying, "You know very well that you performed well; that you are good. You will miss medicine! You will miss it! You are making the worst decision of your life!"

Elisabeth had met her future husband, Martin Herz, the previous summer in Alpbach in Austria's Tyrol. She had been going there every summer since 1947 to attend what was then called the Austrian College and which today is known as the European Forum. It was founded in 1945 as a meeting place for students and intellectuals by a group of survivors of Austria's World War II resistance movement. Alpbach was one of the most important parts of Elisabeth's life because it was a place to finally speak freely after the war and to meet other Europeans to compare experiences and dreams for the future of Europe.

Martin Herz was born in New York, the son of Austrian parents. He had attended *Gymnasium* in Vienna and then did his undergraduate work at Columbia University in New York. He joined the U.S. Army in 1941 and served in Europe. After the war was over, he was assigned to Vienna to help set up the American headquarters in the occupied city. He left the army a major in 1946 and joined the American foreign service. His knowledge of Austria was extensive and his German language fluent so he was immediately assigned to Vienna, where he served from 1946 to 1948.

In the summer of 1956, he was in Alpbach on vacation from Phnom Penh, where he was at that time assigned. It was August and he knew that all his Austrian friends would be there. When he and Elisabeth were introduced, she thought he was an Austrian.

"It was just one of those things," she remembered, forty-five years later. "He wasn't married, I wasn't married. We were both totally devoted to our professions. He was in Alpbach for seven days and then he had to leave. Before he left, he asked, 'Are we now engaged?' It was very strange. One cannot even say that it was a *coup de foudre*. It wasn't this. It was just that, from the second or third day on, we both felt that it cannot be differently. There is absolutely no question; it cannot be differently."

They were married in Bangkok in the apartment of the American consul-general, who was a friend of Martin's. None of their family members attended, but the Austrian ambassador to Thailand was present, at Elisabeth's father's insistence. The ambassador also hosted a luncheon for the couple after the ceremony. Their wedding trip included a visit to Angkor Wat in Cambodia and an introductory car trip through twenty-eight of the United States, which culminated in attendance at a performance of *My Fair Lady* starring Rex Harrison on Broadway.

Martin then traveled to Washington, D.C., to brush up on his Japanese at the Foreign Service Institute (FSI)[1] in preparation for his onward assignment to the American embassy in Tokyo. Elisabeth returned to Vienna to sit for her medical boards. They met up again in Washington, where Elisabeth was naturalized, and then they flew to Japan.

Elisabeth K. Herz, M.D., had become an American foreign service wife. She was thirty-one years old and spoke little English.

*   *   *

The foreign service that Elisabeth married into in the 1950s was vastly different from the one that Prabhi knew in the 1980s and 1990s and that exists today. In those days, no woman, much less a foreign-born woman, could be a foreign service officer after her marriage. Tandem couples, cases in which both husband and wife are officers, were unheard of, though they are quite common today. The only married women in the foreign service community were the wives of male officers.[2] They were evaluated on their husbands' work performance reports, and the woman who held sway over them all was the ambassador's wife. Men wanting to marry foreign women were obliged to submit their resignations from the service pending the results of investigations into the women's backgrounds.[3]

*   *   *

When Martin and Elisabeth Herz arrived in Tokyo, the wife of the ambassador there was one of the infamous "dragon ladies" of the old foreign service. She liked to keep a tight rein on "her wives." They were expected to be standing by at her beck and call, and anything that distracted them from their embassy duties was frowned upon. It was perhaps inevitable that after a while Elisabeth attracted her unfavorable attention.

"My English was poor and I hardly saw Martin the whole first year of our marriage," Elisabeth said. "He was known for working not only 100 percent but 150 percent, and was chosen by the ambassador to work on secret negotiations for a Japanese-American security treaty. We had to follow the normal daily routine, then, in the evening, Martin would quickly change, sometimes in the office, and go to wherever the negotiations were being held. After the meeting, of course, the ambassador would go home, but Martin had to write it all up so that it was on the ambassador's desk in the morning.

"One evening pretty late, the ambassador's wife called me and said that she just wanted to let me know that our husbands would be out much later than expected. I said: 'Well, it's a difficult time for our husbands and for their wives.' She blew up; she absolutely blew up at me. Finally, when she ended her tirade, I said good night. The next morning, the [Deputy Chief of Mission] DCM's wife called to talk to me. She said, 'You have to apologize.' I said, 'What for?' She told me that I didn't have the right spirit; I had no right to complain, I obviously didn't know what service meant, and on and on. I still refused and then she said, 'You are really doing harm to your husband's career, and you don't want to do that. Besides, you are doing all these other things and not participating fully inside the group.'"

There were apparently two points of contention. First, Elisabeth and her husband had chosen not to live in the high-rise apartment building where most of the embassy families lived, but had found a traditional house in a Japanese community. Second, Elisabeth was volunteering her medical skills at two local hospitals. One was a Japanese ob/gyn hospital where, after initial reluctance on the part of the chairman, Elisabeth was welcomed with open arms when she mentioned that she had trained under the famous Professor Antoine in Vienna and knew how to operate a new microscope he had invented and which the Japanese chairman had just purchased. The other was with an international group of physicians, which served the very large non-military foreign community. Elisabeth was delivering babies and performing operations.

"You cannot imagine how difficult this situation was," Elisabeth recalled. "All the wives were afraid of the efficiency report. But I wasn't going to have my spine broken as I had seen Mrs.— do to other women there. I still had to look at myself in the mirror. In the end, I did agree to go and see her.

"A few days later, I kept my appointment and she was completely ice-cold. I said, 'Mrs.—you don't know me at all. Would you please just listen for a few moments and I will tell you a little about myself.' So I told her a bit about my background, including the fact that I was sixteen years old when I had my first interview with the Gestapo.[4] I didn't say it, but I implied that I was not intimidated by the Nazis and I wasn't going to be intimidated by her. And the amazing thing was—and now as a psychiatrist I understand it much better—from that moment on I was her fair-haired girl. All of a sudden, everything was wonderful and I got very special treatment. But, it still didn't mean that I didn't have to be at the residence when all the wives were ordered to be there. I sat through many official functions hoping that the phone would not ring for me, summoning me to a patient going into labor.

"I made some very good friends among the women I met in Tokyo. One was the wife of a colleague of my husband's. She offered to tutor me in English and we have remained friends ever since. The others were the wives of diplomats from other countries: India, Italy, and Austria. But I could not possibly have stood it there without medicine, and my husband was really wonderful about it all. He was on my side and really took a risk that my activities could be held against him in his efficiency report."

*   *   *

The era of the "old" foreign service is generally accepted to have ended in 1972. The Directive on Wives published by the State Department in that year put an end to the wives' mandatory participation in embassy social life, official calls, and service as unpaid helpers to the ambassador's wife. Since then, a wife has been free to follow her own desires, governed only by general rules of personal comportment abroad, her family's requirements, and whatever agreement she and her husband reach about her participation in his job-related activities.

The directive has been referred to as the "firing of the wives" or the "freeing of the wives," expressions which indicate the division that it caused. Not all ambassadors' wives were dictatorial and, in spite of the obligatory nature of their roles, many women had felt a sense of pride and purpose in helping their husbands and in serving the interests of the

United States abroad. For others, this change was a relief. They much preferred to negotiate their roles with their husbands than to be ordered about by an ambassador's wife.

In spite of the directive, the work didn't disappear. Community activities still needed organizing, and official functions had to be hosted and attended. The only thing that changed was that the women could not be forced to do any of it. If they did choose to contribute their time, they received no official recognition.

Most women want to see their husbands succeed and are, within reason, willing to help them where they can. Today, many complain that, while their husbands may appreciate their efforts, the Department doesn't properly recognize what they do. They don't want to be rated, but they do want their efforts to be officially acknowledged in some way. Rather than feeling part of the mission, they feel like part of the impedimenta.

So, what is the role of a wife in today's foreign service?

In an article written in 1981, Dr. Elmore Rigamer (a State Department psychiatrist who later became the director of medical services in the State Department) described how wives affect community life overseas. Twenty years hence, it is still a fairly good description of the basics. Apart from supporting their husbands personally, he wrote, "[t]he women assume the responsibility of structuring most of the social life in the community; they are involved in the working of the school, itself an institution that is decisive in determining the morale of the post; they stimulate interest in the host country culture and organize enterprises that contribute to the social welfare associations of the cities where they live; and, perhaps most importantly, they make an enormous effort to welcome and settle in newly arrived families…By generously sharing aspects of their lives and interests with persons with whom they come in contact, many wives provide rich personal experiences of what life in America is all about in a manner that is incalculably more effective than what is accomplished by organized propaganda efforts."

He went on to say, "The Department had an opportunity to appreciate these many facets of their work when official families [the wives and children] had to be evacuated for security reasons from several of our embassies in 1979. With the abrupt disappearance of all these functions, the very fabric of the community disappeared. The country of assignment was no longer regarded [by the men] as a place to live and work.

"An attitude developed [by the employees left behind] that one's stay was quite temporary, the post was not home but a place where one put in his days and waited for the next time he was eligible to leave for family visitation. A 'wait it out' mentality prevailed. An incidental observation was an increase in functional or psychosomatic concerns, an oft-encountered symptom in men living alone."[5]

Today's foreign service wife would probably add that she must serve as a transportation agent, orchestrating the family's moves; that she must attempt to raise secure children while moving them from country to country; that she often must find paid employment that uses her education and contributes an increasingly necessary second income for her family; and that she must otherwise create a fulfilling life for herself as she follows her husband's career path.

While wives continue to contribute their time and energy to the creation of community abroad, they are less inclined to define themselves by their husbands' positions in the foreign service than by their own talents and goals. To the extent possible, they are striving to have lives of their own. For the foreign-born wife, figuring out her role in the foreign service is only one of the issues she has to deal with after she marries.

Jennie's Story

Life in the "Big Apple City"

Jennie arrived in New York in 1988, when she was in her mid-twenties. The second of four children of a Taiwanese military officer, she had attended a Catholic high school in Taipei. After graduation, she worked as a jewelry designer for a trading company in Taipei, whose owner helped her to get a visa to the United States. Through a high school friend, she found a place to stay in New York.

She signed up for classes at the Fashion Institute of Technology and also worked a few hours a week in a travel agency owned by a friend of a friend. Her English was far from fluent, but much of the agency's clientele was Chinese and spoke Mandarin, Jennie's mother tongue. She did not have much money and struggled to cover her expenses. Even so, her work-mates at the agency warned her that charging double the normal commission on the two tickets to China that she sold one day would come back to haunt her.

The customer to whom she sold the tickets had been born in China. He was traveling back there for the first time in thirty years and would be taking his twenty-three-year-old son with him. The son, who accompanied his father to the travel agency, had been born in the United States and spoke little Chinese. He didn't say much during the transaction. The father paid for the tickets without arguing over the price. Jennie congratulated herself that she had made a "good Chinese profit" taking care of herself in this "Big Apple City."

Several weeks later, the son called the travel agency and asked to speak to Jennie. "I need your help to get a refund on the return part of the ticket," he said. He told her that he and his father had been evacuated from China along with many Americans after the Tiananmen Square killings in Beijing. He and his father now had to reimburse the government for their flight.

Jennie worked out the refund (adding a fee for herself) and thought that that would be the end of it.

A week or so later, the young man called again. He explained that he wanted to thank her for all the help she had given him and his father, and invited her out for lunch. Feeling a bit sheepish at this point, Jennie finally agreed to meet him. "He was nerdy-looking," she recalled. "Wrong hair-cut, wrong clothes, wrong glasses." She was a design student and considered herself a fashionable young woman with a certain image to maintain. She did not want her friends to see her with him, so she arranged to meet him where she knew none of them would see her.

Over lunch at McDonald's, Jennie discovered someone special behind the unfashionable exterior. "He was a really intelligent and sensitive guy, studying for his doctorate in economics at Columbia University. We talked for a long time," she said. He told her about his family and the impact the China trip had had on them. He talked about the demonstrations, the hostility of the crowds as he and his father were hurried onto buses to leave the town where they had been staying. He told her about the dissertation research he had had to leave behind. He also told her about a conversation he had had with an American embassy officer during the flight home. They had discussed foreign service life and the opportunities for a career. The young man liked what he had heard and when he got back to New York decided to leave his doctorate program and switch to international relations, with plans to join the foreign service himself.

Jennie already had a boyfriend, but she and the young man kept in touch, and over time became good friends. He finished his second master of arts degree, sat for and passed the foreign service exam and moved to Washington, D.C. They talked on the phone from time to time but after a year had passed without any contact, Jennie called his mother to find out where he was and to get his phone number. She learned that he had been assigned to Georgetown, Guyana. Jennie wasn't sure where that was, but she called anyway. He invited her to visit for the Marine Corps Birthday Ball in November, the social highlight of the year in American embassies and consulates. She had broken up with her boyfriend by that time, and accepted his invitation. A special waiver had to be requested from the Guyanese government to get her a visa because Taiwan and Guyana did not have diplomatic relations.

She made the trip, which reestablished the friendship, and after she returned to New York they kept in touch, now more than friends. But when he proposed, she hesitated. Their backgrounds were so different: his parents were academics and well-off; her family was of modest means. Not only that, she was three years older than he, and in Chinese culture this is not the ideal. When they eventually did marry in 1995, she was 31 which, according to Jennie, is over the hill by Chinese standards.

By that time, her husband had been assigned to Shenyang in China, with an onward assignment to Beijing. Jennie visited him in Shenyang, but they started married life together in Beijing, six years after she had sold him and his father their tickets for the first trip to China. One day, she summoned up the courage to tell him about the exorbitant commission she had charged them. His reply was, "Good job, honey!"

Chapter Two

Transitions

Biographers of Marie Antoinette describe the scene at the border where, as a fourteen-year-old archduchess, she passed from her native Austria into France to assume her role as wife of the heir to the French throne. The Parisian and Viennese court protocol experts had ordered a wooden pavilion to be built on a small, uninhabited island in the Rhine. The pavilion contained a ceremonial hall with an antechamber on each side—one facing France, the other, Austria. The young girl and her entourage entered the room facing the Austrian side of the river, where she was stripped of all her Austrian clothes and jewelry and dressed in French-made garments, everything from underwear to shoes. When she was ceremoniously handed over to the French officials and led through the second antechamber into France, she had nothing and no one from her own country with her. Reportedly, the first thing she did was burst into tears. It was not a great beginning, and one that was followed by an unhappy marriage, a troubled life, and a violent end.

While less dramatic, the experience of any woman who leaves her own country to live in her husband's homeland mirrors this act of shedding: leaving the old and familiar and taking on the new and foreign. Twenty-first-century psychiatrists would undoubtedly advise against the wholesale shucking of the past that Marie Antoinette attempted, which also included her declaration that she would henceforth speak only French instead of her native German. A healthier approach is to strike a balance between the desire to fit in and the need to maintain identity. For the woman who marries an official representative of another country, whether a king, a prime minister, or a member of the diplomatic service, the pressure to assimilate is strong because by virtue of her marriage, she is seen as a representative of the country herself.

A woman can fit into a community by figuring out what the rules are and behaving in accordance with them. Assimilation is another matter and can take a long time to complete, depending upon whether she spends enough time in one place to feel at home and establish roots. To become an American is to assume a civic identity, not an ethnic one, and the population of the United States is made up of people from many countries and ethnic groups. But there are still ways of behaving and looking at the world that are typically "American" and which are absorbed over time rather than acquired by flipping a switch. One woman told of being visited by a cousin in her Virginia home after she had lived there for a few years. He went home and told her family that she had become very American. She was puzzled about what he had seen in her to prompt such a comment.

There are two American communities to which the foreign-born foreign service spouse must adjust after her marriage: one is the embassy community overseas, and the other is the wider community in the Washington, D.C., area (the District of Columbia, Maryland, and Virginia). Most of the women I talked to started married life in one or the other.

My own experience was somewhat different because my husband and I had been married for nine years before he joined the foreign service. We met in Washington, where he was living and where I had gone to work for the World Bank. Like many young Australian women of my generation, I had left Australia on a working holiday to see some of the rest of the world before returning to settle down. I was twenty years old when I left Sydney and planned to be away for about two years. When I arrived in Washington in the fall of 1967, I had already been gone one year, which I had spent in England and Europe.

I shared a house in northwest Washington with four other young women—three Americans and one Briton—and from the beginning felt quite at home. I don't remember going through the culture shock I have experienced in other countries since then. But my first full year in the country, 1968, was an eventful one. Martin Luther King Jr. and Robert F.

Kennedy were assassinated; rioters looted and burned 14th Street, and the National Guard was called into the streets of Washington. President Johnson announced his decision not to seek reelection and Richard Nixon was elected president. It all happened against the background of the war in Vietnam.

I met my future husband in November of 1967. He had graduated from college the previous June and was scheduled to report to the Marine Corps Officer Candidate School in Quantico, Virginia, the coming January. We saw each other often from November until January and, after that, when he took weekend leave to his parents' house in Maryland. We announced our engagement in August 1968, a month before he left for Vietnam. I stayed in Washington until he was due for his five-day R & R (rest and recreation leave) in May 1969. He requested Sydney, and two months before he was to arrive there I flew home to help my mother arrange our wedding. He arrived on a Monday morning, we were married on Tuesday evening, and he left the following Sunday to return to his infantry unit near Danang. I remained in Sydney and went back to work at the publisher's office I had left in 1966.

My husband's thirteen-month tour was up in October 1969, and when his flight reached Guam, he called to tell me he was finally, safely, on his way home. Forty-eight hours later I said good-bye to my family and got on a plane for Hawaii, where we had arranged to meet. It was the day I had been waiting for over many anxious months, but I cried most of the way to Honolulu. We spent a week there before returning to Washington. He had been assigned to teach newly commissioned officers at the Marine Corps Basic School in Quantico, so we started married life together in an apartment in Woodbridge, Virginia, between Washington and Quantico. I went back to work at the World Bank until just before our first daughter was born in 1971.

When my husband's three-year commitment to the Marine Corps was up, we moved to Boston, where he attended graduate school. We lived on the G.I. Bill and what I earned temping and typing papers for professors and other graduate students. After two years there, we moved to the Caribbean island of Trinidad for my husband to do his doctoral research. We stayed there a year, then moved to Miami, where he had a teaching position. Our second daughter was born in Miami in 1975.

In 1976, my husband joined the foreign service, so we moved back to Washington. By the time he received his assignment to India in 1978, we had moved seven times in nine years. A two-year assignment in New Delhi sounded positively settled to me.

By the time we left for India, I had already made the transitions to marriage and motherhood, worked through the periods of homesickness, come to terms with living far from my own family, grown accustomed to life in the United States, and become an American citizen. I cannot imagine having to do it all at once, as well as having to learn the language, but that is precisely what many of the other foreign-born wives have had to do.

Arriving in a new place is like becoming a child again because you have to relearn the most basic skills. You have to memorize a new address and phone numbers, figure out the currency, find your way around a new city, and get home again. There is a lot of information to absorb. What are the rules in this new place? How does the supermarket work? Do you bag your purchases yourself or does somebody else do that for you? Are bags even provided at all? What does the cashier mean when she asks "Flaschensettl" (in Vienna, Austria) or "paper or plastic" (in Vienna, Virginia)? How do you pay on the bus or the tram or the subway? What clothing is appropriate? Should your arms and/or legs be covered? Can you wear your exercise gear in a department store and expect to be waited on politely? How do you use an ATM machine? How does an automated gasoline pump work? When you make a phone call, what is the difference between a ringing tone and a busy signal? Can you wash your car on Sunday without the neighbors calling the police?

All small things, but added up they can make you feel less than confident as you navigate a new situation. You are in a strange new place and you have no friends. When there's a language barrier, the simplest tasks of asking directions or arranging for a plumber to come to the house become large problems. Usually, in time, a comfort level is reached and life goes on.

Some of the women traveled immediately after their marriages to another foreign posting with their husbands, and some moved to the United States for an assignment in Washington. Although the husbands come from all over the United States, Washington is where they must work on a home assignment because that is where the foreign affairs agencies are located. The two experiences of transition are vastly different from one another.

Assignment Overseas

The foreign-born foreign service wife has two cultures to navigate overseas—that of the American embassy community and that of the country itself—but in some ways, overseas is easier. In an embassy community, a support structure is in place for the woman to use. On arrival, newcomers are usually met by a sponsor, whose (volunteer) job is to welcome them and introduce them to other members of the embassy community. In most embassies, a community liaison office coordinator (CLO) is responsible for monitoring the morale of employees and their families. Living quarters, even if temporary, will have been organized either in a hotel, an apartment, or a house. There is usually a women's organization that provides opportunities to meet other women, and a school where parents can meet other parents. The American community is reduced to a manageable size, depending on the place of assignment. Typically, the community at a hardship post will be more supportive than one in a large European city.

Also overseas, American-born wives are foreigners in the countries of assignment and share this experience with the foreign-born women. The husbands also are not at home, so there is no hometown advantage in the relationship. If the local language is the woman's mother tongue, she has a decided advantage in the host community. But even with proficiency in

English, some women have found it difficult to adjust to an embassy community.

Jennie, from Taiwan, had lived in the United States for several years and had experienced American culture. After her marriage in 1995, she had to adjust to the culture of the foreign service. She remembered, "I didn't even know what a foreign service officer was. When my husband first went to Washington before we were married and told me he was joining an 'A-100 class,'[1] I thought he was saying '1-800 class' and that he was working for the telephone company! When we decided to get married, he told me that because I was not an American citizen, I would have to go through a background investigation. The investigator came to the college where I was studying, and I had to ask the dean for the use of a room for the interview. It took three hours and was not a pleasant experience.

"My husband was already assigned to Shenyang, China, at the time of our marriage. I was finishing my degree in New York, so I traveled just to visit him and then to pack out for the move to Beijing. By that time, I already had a green card, but I still traveled on my Taiwanese passport. I had to go to the Chinese embassy myself to get my visa for China. I had a paper from the U.S. consulate in Shenyang, which identified me as the spouse of a U.S. foreign service officer. It was complicated, but I got the visa.

"Shenyang was a really small and depressing place: no airport terminal, just an open area and soldiers with machine guns directing people. All the consulate employees lived in one apartment complex. Each time I went to Shenyang I had a good time, but the only thing my husband and his friends talked about was their work. I had no clue what they were talking about and always tried to change the subject.

"When I came back from Shenyang, I went to Washington for my naturalization so that I would have a diplomatic passport for the Beijing posting. I arrived in Beijing without any orientation. I didn't really know what an embassy was all about or what we were supposed to do. I didn't even have a security briefing until I had been there two years.

"The first year in Beijing was very difficult, mostly because of my husband's work hours. I was still newly married and struggling to understand the system of the foreign service. From the day we arrived, my husband was constantly working. He was an economics officer there, so during trade negotiations he would be working twenty-four hours a day. He didn't mind, but I did. So much work for so little salary."

Didem, who is from Turkey, met and married her husband in 1984 in Istanbul, where she was working as a private secretary for a local businessman and he was a communicator at the American consulate. They were both twenty years old. After their marriage, they moved to Monrovia, Liberia. "The first year was really tough," she remembered. "I am very close to my family and I was homesick. I didn't see much of my husband because he was either traveling or working shifts. When he was home he was sleeping. It was very lonely for me. It seemed as if everyone was working and didn't have time for anything else.

"There were no jobs available for me the first year, so I spent my time exploring Monrovia. I took taxis because I didn't know how to drive. I never needed to learn in Istanbul, and we didn't have a car in Liberia anyway. There was an international women's group but the women were mostly older with interests that were very different from mine. Meetings were crowded and it was hard to talk to anyone. The second year, I found a job in the embassy post office, and that helped me to get to know people. Every day we had to go to the airport, and I had a really adventurous and interesting time. It was much easier after that and I was no longer lonely.

"After our two years there, we took leave in the U.S. and then moved to Ethiopia for two years. Those were wonderful years. Almost all the spouses were foreign-born: Sri Lankan, Pakistani, Norwegian, and Latin American. We entertained a lot, including TDYers [temporary duty officers] who passed through frequently. The United Nations was there, so we did a lot of things outside the American community as well. We lived in a compound because of the political situation in the country, but we still managed to have a group of Ethiopian friends. The first day we were there I heard the CLO position was open. I applied and got the job."

Inger is Danish. She and her husband met in a Copenhagen hospital, where he was a patient recovering from an automobile accident and she was a nurse. They spent three years in Washington after their marriage in 1971, during which time their son was born. "My husband was assigned at short notice to Madagascar," she said. "When we got off the plane in Antananarivo, I got my wake-up call to life in the foreign service. My husband was sent out as chargé d'affaires and Madagascan government officials were at the airport to greet us. I was twenty-six at the time (I am twenty years younger than my husband) and I remember that I arrived in jeans and pigtails, having been en route (with a small child) for four days because of flight delays. Everybody in the receiving line was groomed to the last hair. You've never seen anybody visit the local hairdresser so fast or have clothes made so fast as I did. I worked very hard at playing my part. I took intensive French lessons to recover the French I had learned in school and was almost totally immersed in social obligations at home or outside."

Susi is from Kuwait. Her father was Kuwaiti and her mother is German-born. Susi met her husband in Kuwait in 1992. She said, "My husband chose a German-speaking post [Bern, Switzerland] after we left Kuwait, so that made a big difference for me, because I am fluent in German. We spent four months with his family between our marriage in the U.S. and moving to Bern, and that was a great chance for us to get to know each other. His parents were extremely supportive, and I have learned a lot from them and I feel very close to and fond of them, but it was nice to get away to start married life together on a more equal footing; it was much more neutral."

Salote left Fiji and joined her husband in Lagos, Nigeria, where they lived on an embassy compound. "It was hard," she said. "I had come from Fiji, where you never stay inside. Then I got to Nigeria, where I was not supposed to go out of the gates by myself. If we went out shopping, we were supposed to go in a group in an armored vehicle. But the people in the embassy were really nice. The women had a sewing group that met once a week. They invited me to join them and taught me how to cross-stitch. I had never done any sewing; I'm a working girl. (When I finished high school in 1974 I went straight to work. By the time I met my husband, in 1985, I was in charge of the commercial side of the Bank of New Zealand in Suva.) But I found that I enjoyed cross-stitching, and it's something that I continue to do. I was very shy in the beginning. My husband was always pushing me to try and participate more. In the bank where I worked in Fiji, I was very outspoken, but there I was in my own place. I was used to Australians and New Zealanders because I worked with them, but I wasn't used to Americans. There's a big difference. Plus, I had never lived in a community where I was a minority. But with each new post I became more comfortable."

Assignment to Washington

In Washington, the employee's work does not include the family to the extent that it does overseas. It is as if the family, which is very much a part of the diplomatic representation of the United States abroad, is dismissed until the next overseas assignment. It is presumed that the family members are now at home and can take care of themselves. The employee and his family are responsible for finding their own housing and a foreign service officer leaves home for work each day just like the dentist or the accountant who lives next door.

Any contact with the foreign service women's organization or participation in programs and foreign-service-related classes offered at the Overseas Briefing Center (OBC)[2] is up to the wife. Many wives (American- or foreign-born) see this situation as an opportunity to take a break from being Mrs. Foreign Service Officer and plunge into American life as best they can. Some find their community among other returned foreign service people and keep in close touch. In any case, the only person likely to be waiting at the airport in Washington to greet a returning family is a relative or a friend.

All the women I interviewed spoke of loneliness and homesickness in the beginning. As in any cross-cultural marriage, the couples had to adjust to each other. The husbands often worked long hours and, without friends, the women spent many hours alone. Some talked about exploring the city as tourists; others talked about watching television to learn the language or to become familiar with local brand names of products they needed to buy for their homes. Instead of moving into an immigrant community where they might find support in their own languages, they were single immigrants thrust right into mainstream American life. On the one hand, this was an advantage in that they were forced to learn quickly, but, on the other hand, they risked having their emotional adjustments overlooked because, in comparison with other immigrants, they seemed to have it easy with an educated, employed, American husband.

In this respect and in others, their situation resembles that of the wives of American GIs who came to the United States after World War II. The largest group of war brides was British, and the majority entered the country in New York on ships specially chartered by the U.S. government. They then scattered to their husbands' hometowns all over the country, where any language problems they had were of regional accent and colloquial vocabulary. Many of them did not regard themselves as immigrants because their only reason for traveling to the United States was to be with their husbands, a view shared by some of the foreign service wives. The biggest difference in the two experiences is that the war brides came with the anticipation of making their permanent homes in the United States. A small percentage divorced and went back to England, but the majority remained and settled in communities in the United States and raised their children here.[3] A foreign-born foreign service wife is likely to live in the United States for only two or three years at a time before leaving again with her husband on assignment to another country.

Even though Washington is the only American city they actually live in for any length of time, many foreign-born wives never regard it as their home. Nor, in fact, do their husbands whose hometowns are elsewhere and who also look on Washington as a temporary place of assignment. (Many American-born foreign service couples feel the same way about Washington. When it comes time to retire, they choose to return to one of their hometowns or to some other place.) Not having a permanent home did not bother most of the women. Some of the older ones who were tired out after many moves did express pleasure in being able to unpack and stay put when their husbands retired, and one or two had homes to which they were emotionally attached, but the younger ones were quite happy to move and were not thinking about buying their dream house in a place of their choice until retirement. Houses they buy in Washington are for convenience or as an investment. This willingness to remain rootless was a reflection of their view of Washington as just another post and their desire to go back overseas where they felt life was easier and more interesting.

Even those women who had lived in American embassy communities overseas for years experienced culture shock when they came to live in Washington for the first time. Lesley, who is British-born, remembers moving to Arlington, Virginia, in 1959. She had been married in 1950 in London and served there with her husband, and afterwards in Cairo, Egypt; and Tehran, Iran. She said, "When I first came to live here, I was not a happy camper. I had already lived overseas for a long time and I was used to living among Americans. The place we moved to was charming, but neither of my neighbors spoke to me. The welcome wagon never came near my door, and I had to go more than halfway to orient myself. I joined the League of Women Voters; I joined the local garden club; I joined the Citizens' Association; I joined a bowling league. We only had one car and my husband needed it to get into work, so I would get rides with one of the other women and give her a gift at the end of each session. Now, those people were very nice to me. Ultimately, everybody was very nice, including the neighbors, but they didn't initiate and I was very lonely at first and

I really found it extremely difficult. I cannot in my wildest dreams imagine how the women who don't speak English get along."

Michele, who is French, moved to Washington with her husband in 1969 after several tours abroad. He traveled ahead to buy a house, the couple's first, in Maryland. "The children and I were staying with my parents in Paris, and I remember he sent me a picture of it," she said. "I took one look at the house and burst into tears. I was shocked. The roof was covered with asbestos! I said, 'What is this, a chicken coop?' He thought he had done very well. After two years in Libya in the desert, and before that, Yemen, which is not very green, he had gotten grass. He had bought a magnificent garden and thought it was wonderful. Unfortunately, I couldn't care less about the grass. I just wanted a solid house. Not one that was made of wood and had asbestos on the roof! And it didn't have wooden shutters that I could close at night and make sure that I was going to be private in my own home. I was miserable. I would go every night with safety pins—I had a whole box—pinning the curtains together. Just pulling the curtains was not enough because there would be a crack. I was terrified in the morning when I was unpinning them that the mailman would come. The mailbox was right outside the front door attached to the house. It took me three years to appreciate the fact that I could put my letters out without having to go to a mailbox, but initially, the idea of someone coming that close to my house and maybe looking in my living room was horrifying to me. What an invasion of privacy!

"In French culture you have circles. First is the dining room table where the family gathers, a sacred circle. Then you have the house, another sacred circle, and you have to keep people outside from even looking into it. So you have the shutters. And then, of course, you have a fence around the house with a gate you can lock to prevent people from coming closer. The French defend their privacy with all their might."

Latha had never traveled outside India before her marriage in 1978. She said, "I worked in Madras for USIS [U.S. Information Service]. When I first arrived in the United States, I had a decent knowledge of its history and culture through school, books, movies, the USIS-sponsored cultural events, and the Americans I worked with. I was still unprepared for the reality of it when I arrived at JFK airport in New York. It was so different from what I was accustomed to. I remember looking around the airport and observing immigrants who had just arrived from Southeast Asia stumbling on the escalators. They looked as lost as I felt. It was obvious that they did not speak any English. I took comfort in the fact that at least I spoke the language of this new country and I was better off than they were.

"In the next couple of years in Washington, I adjusted to life in America. I discovered that most Americans were unlike those I had worked with in Madras. Not everyone was as well-read or knowledgeable about the world outside the United States. I tried to become more 'American.' In order to fit in, I had to shed my *Indianness*."

Bo-Yeon is from South Korea. She moved to the United States with her husband after their wedding in the early 1980s and they rented a small apartment in Virginia. She was twenty-six. She said, "Even though I had lived and worked in Hong Kong away from my family for several years before my marriage, I was terribly homesick when we moved to the United States. Hong Kong is really crowded and noisy. Plus I had a job there. The U.S. culture was so different, the land so huge, and I didn't know anybody at all. I had nothing to do—in the beginning I think I vacuumed the apartment four times a day! I would walk or take the shuttle bus from the apartment complex to the shopping center just to see people. I wanted to work, but I didn't know what was available. My husband was too busy to help me look for a job; it was easier for him that I stay at home. I took some aerobics classes and art classes at a community center but, after about six months, I went back to Korea and persuaded one of my younger sisters to come back to Washington with me. My husband and I moved to a three-bedroom townhouse and my sister stayed with us for about a year. Having her there helped me a bit, but I was still not really happy. Then I got pregnant with my daughter and a new chapter of my life started."

Allison is from Trinidad and Tobago. She said, "Before I was married, I had come to the States on vacations. I always loved coming here, but then I knew I was going back home. You have all your friends and all your life there. When I first came here in 1995 after my marriage, I was a little worried. It dawned on me, 'Hey, what have I done! I'm married to the most terrific guy, but this is different. I don't have a job, the country is big; it's scary.' I was very homesick. I missed the food. My husband tried to find restaurants that served hot sauce, but I missed the Caribbean flavor. The only time I was happy was when I went to Queens, New York, to be with my own people, to talk to someone who sounded like I do. Someone to understand when I said, 'Let's go limin'.' From talking to people, I realized that it was a normal thing. Everyone goes through it. If anyone tells you that they never get homesick, they're not telling the truth."

Didem and her husband went to live in Washington for the first time after the Liberia assignment. She said, "When we arrived in Washington, I expected it to be like arriving at a post, where somebody meets you at the airport, somebody cooks you a dinner. I was disappointed and shocked to find that we were really on our own. We ended up in Virginia, where we bought a really nice house, but I found that I didn't like the neighborhood. I was expecting that we would visit back and forth with friendly neighbors, but it was like a ghost city. You didn't see anybody enjoying the beautiful houses or the beautiful scenery. I was the only person in the garden during the day. This is how I saw American people and American life: everybody works, everybody comes home tired, and everybody is sitting in front of the television. I was really sad."

Wati met her husband in Indonesia, her home country. They were married in 1981, and when he was later assigned to Washington, they moved into a house he already owned. "My only difficulty in moving to Washington was that I didn't have any helpers," she said. "I didn't really cook in Indonesia. In my hometown, a middle-income family can always have helpers for a modest salary. So coming back here without any helpers and a little baby at the same time was difficult. I found it very lonely during the day, because a lot of people worked. Even in this row-house neighbor-hood, I didn't see anybody in the morning. That was a shock for me because I came from a busy neighborhood with people coming and going."

Helga, who is from Germany, and her husband spent two years in the Washington area in the 1980s between overseas postings, and for her it was a very positive experience. She recalled, "We bought a house and my first child was born here. I had no problems. I thought it was painless. As well as German, I spoke fluent Spanish and pretty good French, but I had never had a chance to really learn English. So I learned it when I lived here. The beginning was a little bit hard, but the neighbors were great—the whole neighborhood is wonderful here, very child-oriented. I joined a baby group after the birth, very well organized. I think it's very convenient to live here. It's clean, you get everything; health facilities are good: it's very nice. But, I think I wouldn't like to live here forever, I mean not with-out some time in between in Europe."

Tanja is from Croatia and speaks fluent English. She moved with her husband to Washington in 1997. She said, "I felt that I had to come and live in the States for a while. I had already been representing the country overseas (in Croatia and Zaire) and had never lived in it. I wanted to live in the city, but when my husband showed me the parts that we could afford, I said no. We rented a townhouse in a close-in Virginia suburb for a couple of months and searched for a house. The rental house was furnished and cost us around $2,300 a month, so we were in a hurry to move out of there. It was September, which is still hot and humid in Washington, and I was seven months pregnant. We did not want to live too far out of town because my husband didn't want to commute and I didn't want to be stuck out in the far suburbs. We searched every day and finally found a house. When we moved in, I was huge and ready to have a place to call home. I was so happy to just have my things, to put my books around.

"For the first couple of weeks, it was very lonely. My husband's friends in the area were all single and lived in the city, so they didn't have time to chitchat with me during the day. I went sightseeing, although that was tough because I was fairly big by that time. I couldn't really walk for more than a couple of hours. Then we got our dog back and I would take him out to dog parks. I joined an exercise class for pregnant women, which I found through my doctor's office. It was twice a week: clumsy, big women trying to jump and hop. I continued with another class after my daughter was born. I made a few friends among the women there, and we still see each other two or three times a week. They are my closest friends now because they don't work, they are full-time moms, they live close by, and our kids are the same age. One was also in the foreign service and has since gone overseas. I was the closest with her because we had a similar lifestyle and she understood things the other two didn't."

Jennie and her husband stayed in Beijing for three years and then moved to Washington. She found that to be another big challenge. She said, "I love New York; in fact, I missed it so much that when we were in China, we came back every year to visit friends and my husband's family. I had no friends in Washington and, as usual, my husband disappeared to the office as soon as we arrived. I was constantly on the phone to Taiwan and New York.

"I had organized our shipment from Beijing so that our car would arrive in Washington before we did. So while we were in temporary housing, I would open the map each morning and drive somewhere new: Arlington, Tysons Corner, downtown Washington. Little by little, I learned my way around. We bought a house in Virginia and I spent my days unpacking and hanging pictures. I started taking some interior design classes at a local college, and we met up with some of my husband's A-100 classmates. Our daughter was born in 1999 and my mother and sister have since traveled to visit us."

Elisabeth and Martin Herz moved to Washington in 1960 after the Tokyo assignment was over. They bought a house in northwest Washington, which Elisabeth set about decorating. She remembered, "There were certain things I missed about Vienna, particularly serious conversation. I was alarmed to find that intellectuals, people I had revered all my life, were referred to as eggheads in the United States. However, nothing weighed on me to the extent that I was overwhelmingly bothered by it. My priority was to obtain American credentials to practice medicine.

"I had to present all my credentials from Vienna, which is normal, plus sit for an examination set by the Educational Council for Foreign Medical Graduates. To prepare, I studied all sorts of American books. There was an English exam for which my English by then was good enough to pass. Then there were seven hours of multiple-choice questions. I had never in my life seen a multiple-choice question and especially not the kind that said: if (a) and (b) are related, then it's (d), but if (a) and (b) are not related, then it's (c). In Vienna, I had only ever had oral exams, usually for five hours with the professor. In my opinion, you get a much better picture that way because as part of the exam you had a patient present. You had to present a diagnosis and specify what kinds of tests you would have to make to verify the diagnosis. In this way, the professor could see what sort of approach you had with the patient, how you behaved, what response you got, how much contact you were able to establish, all things which are exceedingly important for a physician. In any case, I passed this exam. But then I had to get a license to practice.

"American licenses are not accepted in Austria and Austrian licenses are not accepted in the United States. Applications for a Washington, D.C., license for doctors from countries where there is no reciprocity had to go through a commission. The identities of the commission members were a secret, and I was told by the American Medical Association (AMA) that it was practically impossible to even submit an application. Without a license I would have had to do my internship and residency all over again, which obviously I did not want to do. I was very discouraged, but then I got extremely lucky.

"We had gotten to know some very interesting people in Washington, and one night at a party at our house I was talking with one of them. He observed that I looked 'down in the mouth.' After he explained what that meant, I told him the whole story. When I had finished he said, 'I am one of the commissioners.' I couldn't believe it! He then offered to submit my papers to the commission and, in the end, I got the license.

"After that I worked as a gynecologist at George Washington University Hospital and the Columbia Hospital for Women. I was surprised to find that medicine in the U.S. was not as far ahead of Austria as I had expected it to be. As I had been trained to do, I was doing natural childbirth with those of my patients it suited, while my American colleagues at that time were still using a scopolamine cocktail for anesthesia. They thought I was a Neanderthal, but when I returned to practice after my husband's next overseas posting, they were pushing natural childbirth for every woman.

"So, I had my own life in Washington, immersed in medicine, and was very happy there for three years until my husband received his next overseas assignment and we moved again."

Common Problems

In one or two cases, the issue of individual self-reliance, a prized quality in American culture, was mentioned as a problem. "What's so great about doing everything for myself?" asked one woman, at a workshop at the Overseas Briefing Center (OBC) on transitions.[4] "In my country, we all help each other." In some cultures, doing things just for yourself is viewed as selfish. The extended family is the norm, rather than the nuclear family, which is more common in the United States.

However, the two issues that came up repeatedly in conversations were *driving* and *money*. Many of the women had lived in busy cities where they rode public transportation and did not need a car. It became immediately apparent on arrival in Washington that a car was essential to mobility and independence. Obtaining a driver's license was a priority. In a culture where most sixteen-year-olds are behind the wheel, learning to drive was a major hurdle for the women. They were afraid of the traffic and afraid of getting lost. Many women who had driven in other countries still found driving on the Washington Beltway a daunting experience. (I had learned to drive on the other side of the road, in a car considerably smaller than the typical American-sized automobile, and needed two tries to pass the test in Virginia in the 1970s, at a time when drivers were required to parallel-park. But, after driving in New Delhi and Seoul, where the roads are overburdened with traffic night and day, I think I could drive anywhere.)

Most of the young couples could afford only one car, so even if the women did learn to drive, many found themselves marooned in the suburbs on weekdays because their husbands needed the car to get to work. When the subway was built in Washington and out to the inner suburbs of Virginia and Maryland, some wives had the option of dropping their husbands at the Metro station and using the car themselves.

Michele had started to learn to drive in Bamako, Mali, pushed by her future husband, after their engagement. She got her first driver's license in Washington in the late 1960s. "I was a very poor driver," she remembered. "One night my husband called me from the State Department, where he had been working late, and told me he was taking the bus, which would drop him off at Sibley Hospital and would I pick him up there. I didn't know where that was, but he told me there was a big sign and I couldn't miss it. Well, I never saw the sign. I had rarely driven at night, it was bitterly cold, I was low on gas and cash, and I didn't dare stop and ask for directions. The only road I knew went to the State Department, so that's where I ended up. I finally made my way back home. My husband was already there: when I didn't show up, he had taken a taxi. He was laughing, but I was in tears. It seemed like such a small thing, but I had not met the demands of my role. I had panicked and, against my better judgment, I had left the children asleep in the house to go and pick him up."

Money concerns among the women I interviewed included opening accounts, understanding credit, and discussing money openly. Most of them eventually developed typical family financial relationships, with joint accounts in addition to personal funds. I also heard stories about other foreign-born wives who did not have access to the husband's salary but instead received an allowance and had no idea about the family's investments.

Anna Maria is from Italy. She and her husband kept track of their finances together, but at a workshop on finances held by a CLO at post, she learned that the credit cards and store charge cards she had used for years did not provide her with a credit history because the accounts were in her husband's name. It never occurred to her that although the cards had her name on them, the credit was not hers. The next time her husband was assigned to Washington and she took a job, she applied for cards in her own name.

Susi remembered having problems in the beginning, before she had a green card: "I could not open a bank account in my own name. I had brought my earnings from Kuwait with me but had to stash the money under the bed for the first four months. I felt very strongly that I had to be financially independent. That's my Arab heritage coming through. Arab women grow up more pragmatically, with the possibility of their husbands taking another wife. In the Middle East, at the time of a marriage, the two families negotiate an amount of money that is put aside for the woman in the event of a divorce. It is part of the marriage contract. I did not have that, so I needed to make sure I was able to rely on myself if the marriage didn't work out. I found out that I could only open a joint account with my husband at the State Department Credit Union or the local commercial banks. I starting lobbying the State Department about this and finally, in 1999, the commercial bank that has a branch in the Department agreed to allow non-citizen spouses to open separate accounts if the couple also has a joint account with them."

Dany, who is German, got used to American ways very quickly but found talking about money uncomfortable. She said, "In Germany, you simply don't talk about money, and you would never ask someone 'how will you be paying.' You just wait until the buyer brings it up, or cash or a card is handed over. When I was working in Washington, I had to invent a whole new set of phrases in order to be comfortable asking about money.

It caused me no end of trouble. In fact, the regular use of credit cards for even the smallest amount struck me as strange. Now that I have gotten used to them, I couldn't live without them and I can talk about money just like everyone else."

Learning English

Having to tackle what seems like an endless stream of adjustments, however small, can erode a woman's self-confidence. She may have met her husband on her own turf, where she was highly functioning. Although he may have spoken her language, she held the position of cultural interpreter. When they move to the United States, these roles are reversed and a previously independent woman becomes, at least in the beginning, totally dependent on her husband, especially if she does not speak English fluently.

Anyone who has ever seriously studied a foreign language knows how exhausting it is to speak it all the time, and what a relief it is to be able to lapse into one's own mother tongue. To me, it is like changing from an uncomfortable business suit with nylons and high heels into a loose shift in which you do not have to stand up straight and hold your stomach in all the time. The woman who already speaks English when she marries her American husband has an enormous advantage. If she does not, it becomes her first priority, especially when she accompanies her husband to Washington for their first assignment after marriage. She cannot function as an independent person until she can communicate.

In order to be successful, the woman needs the cooperation of her husband. This sounds like a given, but when a couple's common language is her native tongue, it is easier to slip into that, instead of turning their home life into one long English lesson. "I don't want to be her English instructor," said one young husband at a workshop on cross-cultural marriage at the OBC. And most of the women do not want their conversations constantly picked apart for grammatical errors. For some husbands, speaking their common language enables him to maintain his professional proficiency, but this happens at the expense of her English proficiency.

Some of the women were unable to use their professional training because they lacked sufficient fluency in English. Carmen, from Chile, has a degree in industrial engineering with specializations in management and finance. When she married her husband in 1997 in Santiago, she spoke no English. She said, "His Spanish is really good, even with the idioms. So I had no trouble with the language with him, but he had to translate for me to communicate with his family. After our marriage we came directly to Washington.

"I arrived here on a Wednesday morning. Thursday, I went to a local language institute to take a test to find which level of English I had. It was Level O basic. The following Monday, I started. I went there for a year. The second year, I decided it was time to look for a job. I didn't know what I could do because my English still wasn't great, but I thought I could do something. I took computer classes at the State Department. They have Microsoft Office tutorials on video. I took the tapes, studied them, took notes, and finished all the Microsoft Office. I thought I could do some kind of office assistant work even though I knew at the time it would be boring for me, but I couldn't do anything else because of the language; still no way to use my degree. So I started to work as a temporary office assistant. I didn't know how to type. I knew how to use software, but typing with ten fingers, no. Now I can do it.

"The temp agency was looking for people who speak Spanish. My first assignments were with the International Monetary Fund (IMF), and then I switched to the Inter-American Development Bank (IDB), but there was too much Spanish spoken there, and I was supposed to be working to improve my English, so I went back to the IMF. There, I met a lot of people who had master's degrees and I started thinking that I would like to go back to school. My undergraduate degree was six years, a long time. I didn't want to lose those years and have to continue with boring office assistant work.

"To go back to school, I knew I would have to improve my English, so I started taking classes part time while I was still working. Then I realized that it would take too long to complete the English as a Second Language (ESL) courses, so I decided to stop working and study English full time again. I also took some business courses to learn the vocabulary. I finished the ESL program and have been studying for the TOEFL [English fluency] test, the GMAT [business school entrance exam], and also taking English for freshmen at a local community college. I have been accepted into the MBA [master of business administration] program at American University and will start in a few months. It's two years full time. I think my first semester is not going to be really hard because I have taken most of the courses before, in Spanish. I just need to take them again in English. If we are assigned later to South America, I will have an MBA from an American university, which is well respected. If we are assigned to some other area, I am not going to put all this effort into a third language. Spanish and English will have to be enough.

"The first year I was learning English, going to school was OK but I needed something else. I was a very good volleyball player at college in Chile and I decided I wanted to play again. My husband called around the county and found a clinic for me. He told the coach that I was a good player but I didn't know the language. I joined a group and during practice, I would go last in the line to watch what the others did and follow them. After a while, I made friends and they invited me to play in tournaments. Sometimes I would speak Spanish and the other players would look at me and I would say, 'I'm sorry, but I don't know how to say that in English.' Or else, I would say the wrong word in English. But, who cares, I was playing. I found that I could help the others with technique. I was able to give something. Volleyball was the only thing that I brought from my country that I could use without any trouble."

In Soon, who is from South Korea and has been married since 1972, wishes now that her husband had corrected her when she was trying to learn English. She worked as a journalist before marriage and said that it had never occurred to her that she would not be able to master the English language to the level where she could use it professionally. She said, "My English is still poor. I studied it in school but could not speak it when I met my husband. We met speaking Korean. When we first came to Washington, I took some English classes, but they didn't help that much, so I gave up. My husband did not correct my English; he didn't want to hurt my feelings. Maybe if he had corrected me at the time, my English would have been better. But some people have the ability to learn languages more than other people. I never thought I could not do that. Perhaps if I had started at an earlier age, I might have been more successful. Now it's too late. I feel like a handicapped person because of the language."

Bo-Yeon, also from South Korea, speaks fluent if not perfectly grammatical English. She said, "In my sophomore year of college I started taking English classes at a language institute in Seoul and, later, I spoke English when I lived in Hong Kong. But I think I would have learned to speak better if my husband was not so quiet. He's not a talkative person. I have one Korean friend who argues a lot with her American husband. Her English is much better than mine! Also, I have always spoken Korean with my children. I think I should have also studied English with them."

Learning English has a wider effect on the marriage than just enabling the wife to communicate in the community. Cross-cultural counselors point out that for couples to really know each other, they have to understand each other's languages. Several of the women spoke about how different they felt while communicating in English. Michele described herself as a split person: "You open the French drawer or the English drawer; you can't have them open at the same time. Until the fluency came, I was much more conservative and uptight in English. In French, I was—French! In English, my hands were still. The day that I was able to make a joke in English and people laughed, I thought, 'I've made it.' The difference in humor is another issue. For a long time, I would listen to jokes in English and at the end I'd say, 'Is that it?'"

Helga said that she also is a different person in her native German. "I have a different intonation, a different vocabulary. My family noticed this when they heard me speaking English. When I'm with my German friends from law school, part of me comes back that is never here: I'm with lawyers and I'm speaking German."

Then, sometimes, other languages get in the way.

After Michele was married, she moved to Beirut, Lebanon, where her husband was to begin Arabic language training. "There was an Arabic course for the wives for two hours a day," she recalled. "People said I learned fast, but that was really not a high priority for me at the time. I was learning marriage, I was pregnant, and I was trying to learn English. I remember that when I went shopping in the embassy commissary, I would hide behind the shelves hoping that no one would speak to me and I would have to answer in English. Some people must have thought I was standoffish, but it wasn't that. I was just terrified."

In Soon's husband was assigned to Japan after their first Washington assignment, so she attempted to learn Japanese instead of continuing to work on her English. [Not long ago, I heard about a wife whose mother tongue was Spanish, who spoke almost no English and was attempting to learn Japanese in a class of English speakers to prepare to accompany her husband on his assignment to Japan.]

Foreign-Born Spouse Support Group

Even women whose mother tongue was English or who spoke it fluently experienced adjustment problems when they first came to Washington. In the early 1980s, some of them met to discuss the need for a support group for newly arrived foreign-born wives, and then they lobbied to create one. They decided that the women's organization, then called the Association of American Foreign Service Women (AAFSW), while helpful as a general resource and advocate, was not addressing the specific needs of the foreign-born. They realized that foreign-born wives needed support and advice from those who shared their experiences and could understand their problems. In 1983, they formed the Foreign-Born Spouse Group, which still meets monthly as one of the special-interest groups supported by the AAFSW. The group provides a monthly get-together, usually an informal coffee at a member's house, where the women can talk freely about their concerns and share experiences. Older women whose husbands have retired enjoy keeping in touch with the foreign service and other foreign-born women, and the young ones, some caring for small children away from their mothers and extended families, enjoy the support of the older women as well as the company of women of their own age. New members come and go, using the group as a spring-board to adjusting to American life.

Citizenship

Whether the women had slight or severe problems adjusting to their new lives, a major issue for all of them was citizenship. Should they become American citizens?

At one time, they had no choice. Until 1987, an American foreign service officer's foreign-born spouse was required to become an American citizen as soon after the marriage as possible.[5] Applications were expedited through the Immigration and Naturalization Service (INS) with assistance from the State Department. Today there is an employee in the FLO office whose primary responsibility is to facilitate expeditious naturalization for foreign-born spouses whose husbands are about to be posted abroad.[6] Naturalization is no longer mandatory, however, except for the wives of CIA officers.

Many of the women I spoke to married under the old regulations, but others who married later made the decision to naturalize anyway. Some were quite happy about it, but others described naturalization as an emotionally difficult experience. Some of the younger women chose to retain their own nationalities, at least in the beginning. Some wanted the option of returning to their countries if their marriages did not work out; some did not want to offend their parents; others just were not ready to take this extra step, feeling that they had already given up enough to follow their husbands and that relinquishing their nationality as well was too much to ask. In some cases, the younger wives were influenced by the fact that their husbands were not necessarily expecting to make the foreign service a long-term career. Many women expressed deep emotional attachments to their home countries, but made the decision to take on American citizenship for purely practical reasons: it made traveling easier and was a prerequisite for obtaining work in an embassy.

Hala is from Lebanon, where she met her husband. When she was naturalized, under the old regulations, a French friend of hers was angry with her for giving up her Lebanese passport. Hala recalled, "I was kind of perplexed and said to her, 'You know, just giving up a passport doesn't give up an identity. Nobody can take away from you who you are. My *Lebaneseness*, if you will call it that, is there. Just because I hand over a passport doesn't mean I've given that up.' And I think this is how I've seen it ever since. It wasn't so much that I was losing something, but that I was adding something to my life that gave me more choice than most people. I have felt that I was able to choose from the American culture things that I liked and also discard what I didn't want to keep from my own culture. Because I don't think any culture is perfect, I felt, wow, I can create my own unique brand of culture that makes sense to me, and that basically is what I have tried to do. America is the land of choices."

Allison and her husband flew from Caracas, Venezuela, where he was assigned, to Puerto Rico for her naturalization ceremony. Just before the ceremony was to begin, the person who was to swear in the new citizens asked Allison if she would make a speech at the end. Flustered, and with little time to prepare, she managed to do it. She remembered saying something like this: "I'm from Trinidad and Tobago and I really love my country. It's very hard to give up my country, but what I am about to do is make this new home my home, and I want to work hard to be a good citizen and contribute something to it."

Without American citizenship, a foreign service wife has to stand in a different line at airports, apply for visas that would be taken care of officially if she were a citizen, and travel without the protections that an American passport provides to citizens overseas. Rekha comes from India. When she and her husband visited France on their honeymoon, she was still traveling on her Indian passport. She said, "The consulate in Madras told me I could get a visa at the airport in Paris, but I could not. The French immigration officials told my husband he had to go to a certain prefecture in the city to get a visa for me. He went off, found the office, and stood in line. Right about the time he got to the front of the line it was time to close for the day. Come back tomorrow. We spent two nights sleeping in Charles de Gaulle airport before I finally got a visa. So it was obvious that it was going to make it easier for us to travel if I also carried an American passport. I didn't have any strong feelings about becoming an American citizen. I may have felt differently if I had been the victim of persecution and the U.S. was some sort of haven, but I had no problem with my native country. It just seemed reasonable to change. I assumed I would spend the rest of my life more closely associated with the U.S. than I was going to be associated with India."

Chris, from England, was married for almost twenty years before she decided to become a citizen. She said, "It was never a problem, but, when I went abroad, I did have to carry with me a quittance form from the IRS [U.S. Internal Revenue Service] in case they would harass me as I was leaving the country about settling unpaid taxes. I also had a letter from [U.S. Agency for International Development] AID's legal department to come and go. If you were away for too long, you compromised your status with your green card.

"When I did become a citizen, I did it in a serious manner, but I regretted it in a way. I was twenty-nine when I got married and I never felt I would successfully become an American. I never felt I was like everybody else. But that doesn't bother me at all any more because Americans come in all shapes and sizes. When I hear my voice on a tape recorder, it's surprising to me that I don't sound the same as everybody else because I actually feel more at home here than I do in Britain."

Frederique, who met her husband in the early 1990s, is French-born. She said, "The day of my naturalization ceremony I felt proud and privileged because I know so many people are dying to come, work, and live in the United States. I also like the fact that being a U.S. citizen makes my life easier. I can work in the embassy and I don't have to deal with INS paperwork, and that makes life more normal and helps me to feel integrated."

There is disagreement, even among the foreign-born wives themselves, about whether a foreign-born spouse should take on American citizenship as a matter of principle because her husband is an official representative of the country. The women who choose not to change believe that their ability to support their husbands in their official duties doesn't rest on whether they are citizens or not, and they are willing to accept the inconveniences created by not carrying an American diplomatic passport.

Whether she naturalizes or not, and whether she starts her married life in the United States or in some third country, a foreign-born wife's transition to marriage and the foreign service is most affected by the attitude of her husband and how supportive he is of her. She has to balance her desire to be with him and to be accepted in his community with retaining those qualities and cultural attributes, which, after all, were a part of what he found attractive about her in the first place.

Chapter Three

Life at Post

The perception many Americans seem to have of diplomatic life, based on novels and movies, is that it is a globe-trotting cocktail party with pay, at the taxpayers' expense. While it is true that diplomats travel widely and have the privilege of experiencing life in other cultures to a degree that tourists' visits don't allow, their lives are not all fun and games. Moving your whole life every few years is no party, especially for the families.

The receipt of orders sets off a chain of events that leads inexorably to the airport. Under the best of circumstances, families have several months to prepare, but some have been known to move at only a few weeks' notice. For the family leaving Washington to go overseas, the list of things to do in preparation reads something like this (there must be some exceptions, but from my observations, in most families this work is done by the wife): Rent the house (paint, repair, and clean, or find someone to do it); schedule and attend physicals for self and children; get all shots required by the country of destination; visit the dentist and orthodontist; collect records—school, financial, employment; counsel fretful children on benefits of moving; sort belongings into four categories—storage, sea freight, air freight, accompanied baggage—in preparation for packing; tie up loose ends—pay bills, return library books, cancel subscriptions; notify post office of new address; inform every personal and business correspondent of change of address; placate hostile teenagers; shop—stock up on clothing if going to an expensive European post, assemble a consumables shipment if going to a post with food shortages; arrange paperwork and vet visits for pets; update prescriptions; reassure grandparents; supervise packing-company employees on pack-out days, and so on.

A foreign service family can usually be spotted easily at an airport. (The largest-size dog carrier is a dead give-away.) Except for the employee, who will probably at least start out in business attire, the family's diplomatic passports in hand, the family members are dressed comfortably, ready for a long trip in economy class. They will be accompanied by the maximum number of suitcases and carry-ons allowed, because packed in those bags are all the possessions they will have before their 700 pounds of air freight catches up with them who knows when. Their sea freight can take months.

At the other end of the journey, an embassy colleague is usually waiting with a vehicle of some sort to transport the family and their baggage to their living quarters, temporary or permanent. The expected period of orientation and adjustment begins and, eventually, a routine develops: employee goes to the office, school-age children go to school, and the wife is left to get on with her life. How well she does this can depend on many things: her desire to be there in the first place; the state of the marriage; how well her husband likes his job; how many evening and weekend hours he puts in at the embassy; how well the children settle in at school and find friends; how well she likes the housing and the furniture the family has been assigned; whether the family's household effects arrive intact; whether the embassy community is welcoming; whether any of the family members get sick; whether she finds work that she wants to do; and whether she finds a comfort level in the host country community, speaking the local language or not. Sometimes, everything hinges on whether she finds a friend.

Our first post was India. In the summer of 1978, we flew from Washington to London where we picked up the old round-the-world Pan Am 001. The flight from London to New Delhi, India, was an aerial milk run with stops in Frankfurt, Germany; Tehran, Iran; and Karachi, Pakistan. On one of the legs, I was seated next to an Australian man, who, it turned out, was acquainted with an uncle of mine who lived in a country town in western New South Wales. A connection of sorts having been made, I expressed some trepidation about the health conditions in India for my two young daughters, who were then six and two years old. He took one of his business cards from his wallet and gave it to me. Hinting at friends in high places, he said, "If you have any problems and the Yanks don't take care of you, just go over to the Australian High Commission and they'll fix you up." I thanked him and pocketed the card. I never had to use it. We ended up staying in New Delhi for four years, and during that time I visited the Australian compound quite often, but usually to play tennis. I was taken care of by the Yanks pretty well.

When my husband first received his assignment to New Delhi, my mother's reaction was, "Oh, dear!" based on health concerns. Our foreign service friends said it was a pity Delhi was going to be our first post because subsequent ones would never live up to it. They were both right. We did suffer continuously from all kinds of intestinal and other health problems, but the embassy community that we found there was a wonderful introduction to foreign service life, and India itself provided endless fascination. Like a first love, a first post can be a special experience. More than twenty years later, we still maintain friendships that we made there.

The ambassador was Robert Goheen, a non-career appointee who had all the qualifications one could want in an ambassador. An academic and former president of Princeton University, Ambassador Goheen was knowledgeable about India and had the respect of both the American and Indian communities. His wife, Margaret Goheen, was a friendly, down-to-earth woman who carried out her duties in a low-key way. They made the ambassador's residence available for community events and invited officers and their families (including very junior ones like us) to informal gatherings there. They and other senior officers, especially the Deputy Chief of Mission, Archer Blood, and his wife, Meg, were strong role models for junior officers and their wives.

When we arrived, we were assigned a temporary house. My first task, unofficial of course, was to find a permanent house. I spent several weeks accompanying the embassy's leasing officer to inspect potential houses until we settled on one that was about to be vacated by another embassy family. After the place was painted and cleaned, we moved in, several months after our arrival. (This was a pattern that was repeated in three of our six posts, with Colombo, Sri Lanka, taking the prize. I looked at forty-nine houses there before I found one we could live in.)

There were no requirements placed on me to do anything, but I watched everybody, trying to soak up as much information as I could, spoken and unspoken, to learn how to fit in and how to function. There were actually three communities I had to learn my way around: the embassy, the international diplomatic community, and the Indian community.

An embassy community is like a little village with all its factions, rivalries, turf fights, and petty squabbles. Inevitably there were some people who complained about everything and should have stayed in the United States. Those I learned to avoid. There were others who flourished, taking advantage of all the community and the country offered. It didn't take me long to realize that it was a good idea to befriend the embassy employee who doled out the furniture or who dispatched the plumbers and electricians. It was up to me to figure such things out, because my husband worked long hours and had little time to be concerned with domestic arrangements.

We got to know our colleagues through the social activities organized around the embassy compound, which included a lively softball league for men, women, and children. The American Women's Association was extremely well organized. As well as supporting social and sporting activities and trips, the members maintained a registry of domestic employees. To run a house in Delhi, a *memsahib* needed a staff. Through trial and error, I learned how to manage a six-person contingent of full- and part-time employees.

My husband was a junior officer, but he was expected to entertain his contacts in government and the private sector, as well as his counterparts in other embassies. Although I had help in the house, I spent many hours shopping, supervising, and organizing family life around representational events. At different times over the four years, I also volunteered at the school, taught sewing to Indian women who lived in a settlement outside

Delhi (and sold what they made), took a part-time secretarial job in the embassy, and traveled around the country as much as my husband's busy schedule allowed.

I met women from other embassies on the tennis courts and through the school, which catered to the international community. We met Indians at official functions or through friends. I don't recall once being made to feel that, because I was Australian-born, I was not a member of the American embassy community. I did receive a few good-natured ribbings from some Australians about being a deserter, but the only times I felt serious pangs were when my husband and I were invited as guests to Australia Day receptions and when, for the first time, I had to apply for a visa to visit Australia on vacation.

I asked the other foreign-born wives about their experiences overseas and whether they had ever been made to feel like outsiders by the American-born members of the community. Some said they had experienced insensitivity, but most of the women said that they had not. They encountered friendly people and not-so-friendly people, but they could not attribute the unfriendliness to their foreignness. Complaints they did have about their experiences in the foreign service were similar to those of the American-born women and not necessarily related to their foreign-born status. They raised some concerns about the rules relating to work for noncitizens but they were considered in a different light (see Chapter Four).

Most of the women believed that their different backgrounds and language skills were an advantage in adjusting to life in other countries and in helping their husbands with their work. They saw themselves as bridges to other communities.

Maria Bauer recalled a dinner party in Cairo in the 1960s where she met the newly arrived Czechoslovak army attaché. She said, "I noticed that when the hostess asked him when he had arrived, he answered, 'Yes.' When she asked how he liked it there, he said, 'Thank you.' It was obvious he didn't understand a word of English. I very quietly started translating back and forth. When the hostess realized that I was speaking Czech, she seated me next to him at dinner. He totally forgot where we were, who I was, and he started to talk. He was very young. I learned that he had spent several years in Russia working in a factory and that he had no military experience whatsoever. When he left after dinner, I mentioned this to the other American guests and, as you can imagine, they found the information very interesting!"

Lesley has served with her husband in London; Cairo, Egypt; Tehran, Iran; Lusaka, Zambia; Khartoum, Sudan; and Bangkok, Thailand; a career spanning thirty-seven years. She said, "I have received respect, interest, and never any form of discrimination in the American community. I shall always adore England, but I'm an American and that's where my allegiance lies. But in many posts, in the local communities, I have found my British background to be an asset. I've always felt quite at home with Australians, South Africans, or with anybody who had any connection with the British."

Bibi accompanied her husband on his posting to New Delhi as counselor for science and technology. She found that the Indians were impressed by the fact that the United States gave the assignment to her husband, a naturalized American. She said, "It was very good for the Indians to see that the United States was big enough and comfortable enough to send Indian-born people like us to represent it overseas. You'd hear: 'My God, can you imagine? You'd never see our government doing this.' I really worked hard at representing the United States in the most gracious manner I could.

"Once, I remember meeting [the late] S. Dillon Ripley, who was then head of the Smithsonian Institution, and his wife at a reception held in their honor at the ambassador's residence in Delhi. I was wearing a sari, as I always liked to do, and when we were introduced, he asked me what country I was representing. I said, 'Yours, Mr. Ripley, but I represent the minorities of the United States.' He held my hand and replied, 'Then you represent all of us, because we are all minorities in the United States.' I thought it was a lovely thing to say and really indicative of the kind of reception I kept getting.

"The American-born employees in the embassy were fabulous. As a wife, I never felt any discrimination in the embassy. The ambassador used my husband's knowledge of the language and country in very positive ways."

One wife did report, however, that during foreign service officer training in Washington, her husband and one of his classmates were taken to task by a female classmate for marrying foreign wives who, she alleged, would follow them around where American-born wives would not. A foreign-born wife must have been looking for a green card, she presumed.

I recalled my own interview in 1969 at the American consulate in Sydney, where my then-fiancé and I went to initiate my visa application the day before our wedding. Although the consular officer knew that I had lived and worked in the United States and had met my fiancé there, she treated me as if our marriage had been cooked up in a Kings Cross motel the night before. But this was before our foreign service days, when he was still in the Marine Corps. During World War II, some American women accused the British war brides of ensnaring American men when they were away from home and vulnerable.[1] Perhaps in her mind I was doing the same.

Michele, who retains a moderate French accent, reported unpleasantness from another quarter. During the Reagan Administration, one of the Cabinet members and his wife visited the post where her husband was the principal officer. As the senior wife, Michele invited all the embassy wives to a tea in honor of the visiting Mrs. Cabinet Member. She remembered, "There was a German, a Filipina, a Korean, and others; I think there was only one American-born wife. At the end of the party with all the ladies, the visitor turned to me and she said, 'There's something that really galls me. We should have laws somewhere forbidding our young foreign service officers from marrying foreigners!' I just stared at her, thinking, 'Wait a minute, lady. Who do you think you are talking to?' I said, "Well, you know Mrs.— there is something about foreign brides: *we* chose to become

Americans; you didn't. You were born into it. So maybe *we* should be given some granny points.' She just looked at me, and then we dropped the subject."

Although the United States increasingly is recognized as a racially and ethnically diverse society, in some places a "typical" American is still thought of as a Caucasian. One foreign service wife, a Filipina of Chinese/Malay extraction, applied for a job as a teacher's assistant in Turkey. The owner of the school, an educated Turkish woman, told her after the interview that although she spoke excellent English, the school really wanted to hire somebody who "looks American."

Other women reported initial curiosity from people outside the embassy but, for the most part, as Helga put it, "No one is coming into your house and saying, 'OK where's the American stuff?' No one expects you to turn yourself into some sort of typical American."

Hala said that at other posts she had always felt part of the embassy family, but at the embassy in Baghdad (their fourth post) she sensed that her being foreign-born was a problem—with the Americans. "During the Iran/Iraq war, my husband was DCM [Deputy Chief of Mission] in Iraq. It was a very difficult and dangerous post. We had SCUD missiles once and then twice a month. We were isolated in the diplomatic community and we had food shortages. Everybody was feeling burned out, including my husband and me, but we tried to hold ourselves together to help people and keep morale up. For example, on Fridays we would open up our residence like a community center so that people could come, bring their games and their papers, and relax outside the office. People liked that. Unlike other embassies, we didn't have a pool or some place where people could gather socially. Occasionally during this period, I felt that when some of the Americans at the embassy were unhappy with the local Arab culture, they were not completely at ease with me. They'd say, 'These goddamned Arabs.' Then they'd turn to me and say, 'Oh my God!'"

Hala continued, "Most of the time, I saw my situation more as an advantage. Having grown up in Lebanon and having traveled a lot, I felt I had a much broader perspective of the world. My family often entertained, so that part of the life was not a big thing to me. I served mostly Lebanese food to guests, with whatever else the cook knew. I'm lucky that just about everybody likes Lebanese food, and in the Arab world people were ecstatic that they could come to an American house and eat the food they liked."

Inger said that she felt that as the young, foreign-born wife of a senior officer, she was being judged harder and that she had to prove herself. She said, "There were jealousies, but that could have been because I was so young and married to the boss. I had traveled extensively; I spoke several languages; I came from a good life in Denmark, not a back alley; and I took to foreign service life quite easily. Because of my nursing, I didn't have to rely on or get my satisfaction through the embassy. I made my friends primarily through my work."

Sangeeta, who is Japanese, joined her husband in Manila, the Philippines, after their marriage in Kobe, Japan, in 1985. She arrived exhausted from organizing the wedding, hosting her husband's family and other American guests, and packing up and leaving home. She said, "My husband had already been in Manila a couple of months before our wedding. After I got there, I basically collapsed with a 104°F fever. But he had to make a previously scheduled trip into the countryside right after I arrived, so initially I was on my own.

"The first year I didn't do much of anything. We had a small two-bedroom apartment with the standard embassy-issue furniture and not much else. It was too hot to play tennis and I didn't want to swim. I gained weight, and my skin got darker and darker. The darker I got, the more I was mistaken for a local. Filipinos are such a mixture: Malay, Chinese. To this day, I'm asked if I'm Filipina or Spanish. This served me well when I went shopping because I got the local prices, but it was a problem for me in terms of security. Even though I had an embassy ID, the local guards would always stop my taxi at the gate of the compound.

"One day, when I was in one of the classified areas of the chancery looking for someone, one of the secretaries came out of her office and yelled at me, 'What are you doing here?' I was wearing my spouse ID but she basically ran me out of there. I was only twenty-four at the time, new, and didn't know how to handle it. I thought I had done something wrong and was in tears. She was secretary to someone senior, and my husband was a junior officer. He said he would talk to somebody about it, but I don't think he did."

Dany's first overseas foreign service post with her husband was to Tashkent, Uzbekistan. She said, "In general, I think I do a lot better adapting to new surroundings because I had traveled on my own before I met my husband and actively chose and pursued this lifestyle. My expectations are very different from some of my fellow (American-born) spouses. I think I am a little easier to please, mainly because I don't expect all things to be American. I have lived without things American before, and I don't miss them as much. On the other hand, I know some foreign-born spouses who are having a very tough time because the America of their imaginations and dreams simply isn't the same as reality. They expected perfection, and the disappointment was intense when it didn't turn out that way.

"Although the questions I had about American life and society have by now been answered, I still remember what my personal confusions and issues were. This means I am perhaps better prepared when a controversial or difficult question is brought up, because more than likely I have heard it before or asked the same questions myself. In the face of criticism of the United States, I might even be more able to comment effectively because I am already very aware of 'outside' views."

A few of the wives preferred that their husbands not accept assignments to their native countries, but others felt quite comfortable about it. Anna served with her husband in her native New Zealand and enjoyed the experience. She had insights into the culture that were invaluable to her husband and, because she had previously served in the New Zealand foreign service, had personal contacts in the New Zealand government. Because she holds dual nationality, she had to pay taxes in New Zealand as well as in the United States. She was called for jury duty towards the end of the tour, but was excused on the basis of her diplomatic status and the fact that she was to leave the country in a matter of weeks.

Tanja met her husband in her home country, Croatia. Four days before their wedding in Zagreb in 1995, the American embassy dependents were evacuated, and the remaining staff members moved from the downtown area to the ambassador's residence. While it had been arranged that the wedding ceremony would take place at the residence, the reception was to be held in a restaurant downtown. With the evacuation, none of the Americans, including the groom, would be allowed to attend. No one was allowed to leave the residence. The ambassador argued the point with Washington and finally convinced officials that the reception was probably safe enough because the restaurant was in a basement. "However," said Washington, "after the wedding, the bride will be an American dependent and therefore will be evacuated to the United States."

"Where?" asked Tanja. "My family is here and so, at this moment, are my future in-laws." In the end, Washington just decided to let her stay in Zagreb.

When her husband's assignment was over, they took home leave in the United States and moved to Kinshasa, Zaire (Congo). After a year there, her husband was asked to go back to Croatia to work with the United Nations (UN) in Vukovar, Tanja's hometown.

"At first we really didn't want to go because we had just unpacked and settled down in a nice house," she said. "Officially, Vukovar was an unaccompanied post, so I was not supposed to be there, but I went because I knew the whole region. Vukovar itself was practically destroyed and I didn't want to live there anyway, so we rented a place twenty miles away and my husband commuted.

"It was a strange year. I was by then an American citizen and a lot of people in that part of Croatia weren't really keen on the UN. They thought it was biased towards the Serbs, which wasn't the case. But people slowly got warm, and it wasn't bad. I didn't feel unsafe but had a strange feeling of being in the middle. The UN was paying my husband per diem for housing and food, but just for him, because officially I wasn't there. Slowly, when they realized that things weren't so unsafe, the other UN guys brought their wives: one from the States, one from Australia, and one from Poland. We would all get together about once every two weeks. Sometimes they would complain to me about things in Croatia and I would say, 'OK, it's not my fault that my country is falling apart. I'm sorry that you can't find things that you can find in the States, but you know, it's just the way it is here.' As I said, an interesting year. But I did get to see my mother a lot because she was still in Zagreb, which was only about three hours away by car."

Two women accompanied their husbands to countries that were traditional enemies of their native lands and found the experience initially uncomfortable. In Soon's husband was assigned to Japan, Korea's former occupier, first in Yokohama and then in Kyoto and Osaka. She remembered, "We were educated that Japanese are bad people, so naturally, I didn't like them at all. I had previously only visited some family members living in Japan. When we lived there, I observed how much faster the Japanese had developed and that they were living more comfortably than the Koreans. I came to understand and admire them."

Besides adjusting to her husband's long working hours in Shenyang and Beijing, Jennie had conflicting feelings about living among the Chinese. She said, "As a Taiwanese, I never pictured myself ever setting foot in China. At first, I was afraid to go out, afraid that when I opened my mouth, people would know that I was from Taiwan and would attack me. Walking down the street in Beijing, I would look at people and wonder which one of them had killed my grandfather. So I kept my mouth shut most of the time, and when I did have to speak, I tried to give myself an accent. When people asked me where I was from, I would say I was from the United States, which was also true. Sometimes I wanted to say,

'I'm from Taiwan and I want to be friendly with you. Please be friendly with me.' Some people would be nice to me, and others, not.

"But I have to say, the longer I stayed in China, the more I loved it. I felt sorry for the Chinese people, especially those of my own age group. Some of them were so intelligent and full of knowledge and ideas, but because of the country's policies, they couldn't go overseas. Compared to them, I felt so lucky.

"At official functions, my husband usually spoke English, but sometimes as a courtesy he would speak Chinese. When they spoke to me at social events, Chinese officials would question me about my husband's background and mine. I got tired of it after a while and made up a different story each time.

"I got a job in the embassy as a staff assistant for the U.S. Customs office. Sometimes I would translate at meetings with the Chinese. Once one of them announced at the beginning of a meeting that they did not want Taiwan to be discussed at all at the meeting. As soon as I opened my mouth, they knew I was Taiwanese. It was very awkward for me but my boss told them, 'She's not Taiwanese, she's American.'"

Jennie also experienced a common occurrence overseas: the Congressional delegation or CODEL. Embassy and consulate staffs are expected to host and entertain visiting members of Congress, their staffs, and, on occasion, their spouses. She said, "I am basically a cheerful and optimistic person, I got to know Beijing pretty well, and I spoke Chinese, so I was given the job of taking care of visiting congressional wives. While their husbands were at work on U.S.-China issues, the wives' mission was touring and shopping. In the last group I showed around, most of the women were polite and friendly, but there was one who really gave me a hard time. She wanted me to bargain for her for even the cheapest items. It was so embarrassing. At one of the palaces we visited, I didn't know the answer to one of her history questions and she said, 'How come you don't know? You're Chinese aren't you?' I also had to pay for my own $30 lunch. After that visit, no more wives."

As they gained experience and confidence, most of the wives made a place for themselves in their communities, sharing the ups and downs with the American-born wives, and deciding on the extent to which they would participate. The older wives mirrored the supporting roles the American-born women of their generation played to their husbands. The younger foreign-born wives seem to share the changing attitudes of young American-born wives to that role. They are making greater demands on the government; they want to be better informed, better supported, and better trained, especially in languages. More and more, their demands center on employment, especially overseas.

Dany's Story

Meeting in Mongolia

Dany is from Wiesbaden, in Germany; her husband is from Texas. They met in Mongolia. "When I was twelve, my family moved from Germany to spend several years in England and I stayed on there to go to university. I studied Modern Chinese at Leeds University and during my second year went to study in Beijing. In my third year, the department offered classes in Mongolian history and language. I took one class, was hooked, and decided to do an M.A. in Mongolian Studies. I managed to visit Mongolia in the winter of 1991 and accepted a job as an English teacher to start the following fall. My job was to teach English in remote settlements to people who otherwise would have had no access to English at all. I spent my first three months with a family in the Middle Gobi before I was sent to Choibalsan, which is the fourth largest city in Mongolia. (At the time it had about 35,000 to 60,000 inhabitants, depending on whom you talked to.) My employers sent me there because the winter was expected to be extremely harsh, and at least in a bigger place they could guarantee my safety and maybe emergency transportation. I already had some friends there who, immediately upon my arrival, were eager to tell me all about the other two foreigners in town.

"On my second day there, I knocked on the door of one of the Peace Corps volunteers and met my future husband. We were married in Germany the summer of 1994. After Mongolia we went to the Solomon Islands with the Peace Corps for a year and then moved to Washington. In 1997, my husband joined the foreign service and our first overseas assignment was to Tashkent in Uzbekistan."

Chapter Four

Work—Paid and Unpaid

The last time foreign service wives were surveyed about their attitudes towards their lives in the foreign service was in 1984 by the AAFSW, with the results published in 1985. Although the survey is eighteen years old, my own observations and the comments of other foreign service wives I know lead me to believe that many of the conclusions reached from the responses to the survey are still true today.

"[The majority] of the respondents enjoy their lives in the Foreign Service because of the opportunities to travel, use languages, and broaden their global outlook through cross-cultural experiences. The Foreign Service continues to offer spouses a lifestyle that is unique, at the forefront of world events, at times exciting, and certainly never dull. . . .The most serious impediments to spouses' willingness to serve abroad are the threat of terrorism, disruption of career plans and family life, and concern about health hazards, especially in hardship posts. . . .*The highest morale is found among spouses who have paying jobs or portable careers, yet who have time to spend with their families and are not overburdened with representational responsibilities...*The lowest morale is found among spouses of Senior Foreign Service employees (my italics)."[1]

While it appears from the survey that the happiest wives are those with paid employment, it was suggested to me that foreign-born wives feel less pressure to work outside the home than American wives do. It is true that a woman's need for fulfillment through paid work is not as strong in some cultures as it is in the United States, and in some countries women's employment outside the home is frowned upon. Susi observed that she often had to defend working in her native Kuwait, but when she decided to stay home with her baby daughter in Washington, D.C., she found herself having to defend that decision. But I think the increase in the desire for, or expectation of, a lifetime career is more a question of generation than of country of birth. The women of my generation were more likely to put aside professional aspirations to follow their husbands than are the young women of today, no matter where they come from.

For wives to have careers in the foreign service is extremely difficult. Work, yes; a career, probably not, unless they want to become foreign service officers themselves and take their chances on tandem assignments with their husbands. If a woman aspires to a profession with an uninterrupted career path, she would be advised to consider marriage to someone other than a foreign service officer.

These days, to hold a paying job is not just a question of desire, it is often a question of need. The U.S. government does not pay dot-com salaries. In 2000, the starting salary for a foreign service officer with a bachelor's degree was $35,000.[2] The government's senior executive service pay was capped at around $135,000. A study published in November 2000 reported that a family of four in the Washington area needed $50,000 for the basics of housing, transportation, food, and taxes.[3] While their husbands are assigned to Washington, many women do find jobs, but some with young children also find that the high cost of day care wipes out any economic advantage such jobs provide and that they are not worth the trouble. Some wives report that short-term assignments to Washington, while their husbands are in language or other training and the family is on per diem, are the most financially difficult times of all.

Foreign service wives also want to work overseas. Spousal employment is one of the greatest problems facing foreign affairs agencies trying to attract and retain employees who are required to work abroad. Increasingly, families expect the government to facilitate that employment. The State Department has negotiated bilateral work agreements with many governments, and has de facto agreements with others.[4] The Family Liaison Office (FLO) publishes information on options available within government and in the private sector, strategies for job-searching, and other assistance.[5] A pilot program introduced in 2000 in Mexico City employed a consultant to help family members find work in the local economy. The results are not yet in as to whether it has been successful.

Short-term employment possibilities overseas include secretarial or clerical work in the embassy; consular associate work (specific tasks within a consular section allowed by law to be carried out by employees other than a "real" consular officer); teaching at the American or international schools or teaching English or other languages to host country nationals; contract work with American corporations or, if the woman is extremely energetic, private business consulting; and the whole range of freelance work of painting, writing, and editing. The Internet has provided increased opportunities for communication and work at a distance. Employment in the local economy depends on knowledge of the local language and the availability of work. Depriving a local citizen of employment is not appreciated and in many countries is illegal. In developing countries, salaries are extremely low.

Some wives reach the decision that their only hope of long-term employment with benefits, social security, and a pension of their own is to join the foreign service themselves. For the foreign-born spouse to do this, she must be naturalized and must have excellent English proficiency, both verbal and written.

Rekha accompanied her husband on postings to Katmandu, Nepal; and Karachi, Pakistan, before joining up herself in the 1980s. She said, "One of the reasons I joined the foreign service was that I was tired of doing secretarial work overseas. I actually took the exam and passed in 1983 but then my kids were really little so I had no interest in working. Back then there was a provision that if you were overseas with a spouse you could defer. When we came back to Washington in 1988, I entered my A-100 class and then was assigned to Bangkok. My husband was able to get an assignment there, as well. I started out in the administrative cone and I did that partly because I knew that the hours would be more regular. I had joined late, at thirty-five, so I was not thinking in terms of how far I was going to go in the service. I switched cones and became a consular officer for tandem purposes. When we had a chance to both get jobs in Katmandu, for a second tour there, the only job available for me was a consular position. I took it and enjoyed the work, and at that point decided I may as well just stay a consular officer. My husband is now retired, so when I am posted abroad next, he will come along as a dependent spouse.

"My present job in Washington is as a management analyst in the executive bureau office of consular affairs, which deals with staffing consular sections overseas, including consular associate positions for eligible family members. There is a significant failure rate [by foreign-born spouses in the consular course] because the material includes legalese and difficult language terms. For someone whose native language is not English, it can be disheartening. I did hear from someone who runs the course that often spouses may not have been that keen to take it, but were pressured by their husbands. The husbands mean well, but it's not easy to pass, and that can't be good for the wives' self-esteem. I have also heard that some consular associates are unhappy because they don't get to do some of the more interesting work. Consular associates are designated to do certain kinds of jobs: visa adjudications. It's not that they aren't competent to do more, it's just that the law hasn't been changed to accommodate them."

Lois, originally from Wales, has spent seventeen years overseas with her husband and has worked inside and outside the embassy. She took the six-week consular course to qualify to work in the consulate in Frankfurt, Germany, where her husband was assigned. The job turned out to be a mixed success. She found resentment on the part of some American employees that they had to give spouses preference over local hires for the positions, and from the FSNs (local employees) who, having spent years working in the consulate, saw wives taking jobs that they considered to be in their line of advancement. She said, "It was a big consular section, dealing with the military. I worked on passports and birth registrations. We had little passport agencies at military facilities and I'd go there and talk to them. Once a year there was a conference and I had to talk about passports for two hours to a hundred military people. A supervisory job became available, so I applied for it. I got it, but it took me a year to get around the local employees.

"In Bangkok, I had great jobs, not in the embassy. An association called Community Services of Bangkok had two programs: one was a relocation program for executives and the other was a program to help people who had come to adopt children, escorting them to hospitals to have physicals and to the embassy to get documents. The woman who ran the programs asked me if I wanted to take them over. For the executive one, I had two or three trainers, consultants I would pick for the jobs. I had a lot of contacts and in the end was also doing real estate for people, finding them homes. The adoption program was wonderful. All the children were special needs children and I would pick the prospective parents up from their hotels and take them to meet their child for the first time at the orphanages. It was very moving, even heartbreaking sometimes. I met some incredible people. I didn't get paid much for the adoption part, but I made up for it with the executive program. So, Bangkok was very rewarding for me in terms of work."

Recently, Lois made the decision to stay behind in Washington when her husband was assigned abroad. She has been accepted into a training program with a Washington investment company. She said, "I am grateful to the foreign service for a lot of the experiences I've had, but I have to say I'm relieved to be out of it, in a sense. When my husband put in his bid for overseas again, I thought, 'I can't.' I'm in my forties now and I want a career. You don't necessarily have to have a career to be a whole human being, but we live in a culture, in the States particularly, where you are labeled by what you do. Also, my husband is getting ready to retire, so I'd better get started on something because we can't live on his retirement with kids and everything else."

For senior wives, employment in the embassy becomes problematic because they cannot hold positions where their performance has to be evaluated by their husbands. Anna Maria served with her husband in

Guatemala twice, the first time when he was consul-general, the second time, when he was the deputy chief of mission (DCM).

She said, "When we went back to Guatemala the second time, my English was pretty good and my Spanish was excellent. I wanted to work, but with my husband being the DCM it was a conflict of interest and not possible. Before I could get upset, an interesting situation occurred. Nicaragua at that time was denying the entry of our consul, and there were many Nicaraguans scheduled to appear for their immigration interviews. So instead of going to Nicaragua, the consul was sent to Guatemala to process the cases. He was not under the direct supervision of my husband in Guatemala, so I could work with him, which I did."

One of the most popular jobs in an embassy for spouses is that of community liaison office coordinator (CLO). He or she is the family member's link, and sometimes ombudsman, to the bureaucracy. The core of this position's responsibilities is morale maintenance. While a long list of standard guidelines covers activities such as post orientation, cultural and recreational programs, dissemination of information, counseling and referral services, and assistance with security, education, and employment for family members, the duties are adapted to deal with what is needed at the particular post.

The CLO has to know the embassy, but she also must know her way around the host community. To spread the (employment) wealth, the job often is shared by two people, with each one being paid for twenty hours a week. Of the women I interviewed, roughly a quarter of them have held the CLO position, sometimes more than once.

Faye Barnes is the director of the Family Liaison Office at the State Department in Washington. Originally from Canada, she has spent almost thirty years as a foreign service spouse, serving with her husband in Venezuela, Spain, Peru, Germany, Mexico, and the United Kingdom. Among her qualifications for this position are the years she spent as CLO in Bonn, Germany; Mexico City, and London. She also speaks Spanish and German. Although originally trained in food science, she found the CLO job more suited to her personality.

"I had done a lot of work with women's clubs in Peru and Germany and found that I really liked that," she said. "I was CLO in Mexico the entire three years we were there. It was important that I spoke Spanish because we had so many foreign-born spouses whose English was not good, not from State so much, but the wives of DEA [Drug Enforcement Administration] agents and those from other agencies. Also, the FSNs [local employees] used the CLO office in Mexico City."

For Allison, from Trinidad and Tobago, being CLO in Caracas, Venezuela, was "a fantastic experience." It was her first post, and she got the job in June of her second year there.

"The best part was working with people, sharing with them, keeping them positive, helping them get oriented to the country," she said. "I think my teaching experience was useful and I was able to help people who were depressed and homesick and going through culture shock. We had over three hundred Americans at the mission to work with. I found that a lot of people who came to Venezuela were overwhelmed and were afraid to go out and make friends. You have to go out and learn the language there, and if you don't you are going to be miserable. It's a natural thing to be homesick, but you have got to put it behind you and not let it govern your spirits. You have to be positive, be productive, and make a contribution. I organized hikes, trips to factories, evenings to the opera, afternoons at the racecourse, and got people more involved in doing things. I started a Spanish conversation class during my lunch hour. The spouses got a lot out of it.

"I organized informational welcome packets, orientations, and coffee hours. We even got two male spouses to go to coffee hours with us. I'm a very friendly person and coming from an island is different from other countries, I believe. We don't care what you look like, if you're green, yellow, or black. A lot of it has to do with how I was raised. I go out and make friends. I get people to talk. I tell them 'Good morning!' twenty times until eventually they answer."

Didem was co-CLO in Ethiopia. Her partner was a foreign service wife from Djibouti whom Didem credits with teaching her about life in the foreign service. She said, "I realized I didn't know much about allowances, so many little things like that. My husband was informed, but I was not. From my CLO experience I learned how to find out information for myself, what training I could get.

"While we were in Ethiopia, dependents were evacuated because of the civil war. We [the CLOs] had to help organize the evacuation, calming down those people who were panicked about leaving. None of us wanted to leave, so it was tough. Most people went back to the States. I had a choice, so I chose to go to Turkey and be with my family. My co-CLO went to Washington, D.C., and worked with the State Department to communicate with everyone. I couldn't have any communication with my husband, who had stayed behind, so she would communicate from me to him, and him to me. After six months, when we were allowed to go back, I was the first there because I was closer. It was the start of the school year, so as soon as I got back I started the processing for the kids who were coming back."

When Salote's husband was assigned to Fiji, her native country, she was hired as the CLO. She said, "When we first went out, we were told that the embassy morale was very, very low. People didn't want to go there, and those who did go just enjoyed themselves and didn't bother about the morale in the embassy. Being Fijian was an advantage for me in the job. I got some good deals for the embassy. I'd start negotiating in English, but when I would automatically turn to Fijian, the prices came down. We were able to do some wonderful things: trips to all the favorite resorts at a discount, hiking in the bush. Everyone was really into it. And that's wonderful when you are a CLO. I always tried to include the local people, the FSNs. It was nice; everybody got along well."

Sangeeta taught Japanese history, politics, and government at the university in Manila, the Philippines, during her husband's first assignment. In Beijing, their second post, she took the CLO position and, by working in the embassy, got over the feelings of intimidation she had experienced as a new wife in Manila. She enjoyed helping people and using her Chinese language. She had taken classes with her husband in preparation for the assignment and, by that time, she had 3+ Chinese.[6]

Wives who are not American citizens have to be creative when it comes to employment. Susi applied to work in the embassy in Bern, Switzerland, where her husband was assigned soon after their marriage.

"Because I was not an American citizen, I was not 'an eligible family member' so couldn't take the jobs that were available for spouses," she said. "After we had been there a year, I thought, 'OK, I'm fluent in German and I know something about Switzerland. I'll try for the jobs that are for non-family members and are open to everyone.' So I applied for full-time jobs as an FSN in the Administrative Section, then later in the Consular Section. In Switzerland, local salary rates were very high. When they offered me the job as an FSN, they wanted to pay me the lower 'eligible family' rate. I said, 'No way, thank you. It's an FSN application. You didn't want me as an eligible family member, so you can pay me as an FSN.' They ended up having to pay me at the higher rate."

Wati, also not a citizen, found work with international organizations at the posts to which the Agency for International Development (AID) assigned her husband. "I worked part time," she said. "I did cost-of-living survey work in almost every post. I also worked as a secretary at the World Health Organization (WHO) in Suva, Fiji, at the United Nations Development Program (UNDP), and the World Bank."

Dany, who has retained her German citizenship, is philosophical about the job issue: "Clearly it is easier for American spouses to land positions at the mission, which is understandable, because of security clearances. So, I guess this is not really a 'foreign-born,' but a 'foreign spouse' issue. In Tashkent [Uzbekistan], a number of naturalized foreign-born spouses have jobs in the mission. It would be difficult for me to get a job here, for a variety of reasons. First of all, the embassy is fairly small, and there are not that many available jobs to start with. Then, most of the jobs that are open to spouses need a clearance, which I wouldn't get because I'm not an American citizen. And thirdly, I would be disqualified for most non-cleared jobs because of the nepotism issue, as they would fall under my husband's supervision.

"I did not come to Tashkent expecting or even hoping for a job at the embassy. I was fully prepared for a job search on the local economy, with foreign companies, and even with foreign missions. Maybe I will feel differently in future assignments, especially when there are no bilateral work agreements, or if other restrictions are placed on me. I think it would be useful to include in the post reports what the job opportunities are for non-American spouses. We are going to China next. I am very excited about this opportunity, as I studied Chinese and I have lived in Beijing before, but there are a lot of questions that have not been addressed, including what my status will be. Diplomatic status will affect what kind of work I can do there."

Some foreign-born wives are at the added disadvantage of not having their professional qualifications recognized in the United States. Helga was a lawyer in Berlin when she met her husband there. She said, "My specialty was youth crime and criminology. I was a public prosecutor in a department where they took care of families, problems with teenagers or youngsters, or where the parents couldn't take care of the kids and they had to take them away. After I finished there I joined a partnership as a lawyer and worked at that for three years before I got married.

"The first time we came to the States to visit, by chance we went to see a movie with Robert Redford about lawyers. I remember coming back to the hotel and crying and saying to my husband, 'You know, it just hit me that I actually cannot be married to you and go on with my law career. It's impossible. Not like somebody who lives in one country and stays there.' But really, I knew that when I made the decision to marry. The skills I learned as a lawyer have helped me in other work, such as the nursery school I founded and ran in St. Petersburg [Russia]."

Tanja is a doctor, but has not been able to practice, even in her home country. She graduated from medical school in Zagreb in 1982, but because she has a Serbian last name, no one would hire her. She finally found work with the Croatian army outside of Zagreb, but after three days she was told they could not employ her, so she went back to Zagreb. She was eventually hired by the U.N. High Commissioner for Refugees (UNHCR) in December of 1992, starting as an interpreter and then working as a medical translator, evaluating cases of Bosnian refugees for resettlement. When she moved to the United States, she found that her credentials were not accepted here and that she cannot practice unless she does several more years of study and is certified. Because she will not be living in the United States for more than a year or so at a time, she has decided that that is not an option. If she did become certified, she still would not be able to practice in the countries to which her husband is assigned, except in some places as a volunteer.

She said, "I did volunteer as a doctor in Zaire, but under supervision. I helped in a clinic, which was run by an American and served Zairians and expats. There were two programs, one for people who could afford to pay and one, basically run by nurses, for people who couldn't pay to see a doctor: simple cases like malaria. They wanted me to have tropical medicine licensing, which you can only take in Brussels to be valid in Zaire. It lasts four months and I don't speak French, so I didn't want to do that. The work that I did there was interesting, though. I saw cases that in medical school I never really paid attention to because I thought, 'Where on earth am I going to see that?'"

Given the choice between doing clerical work for low wages in the embassy and volunteering their professional skills, many foreign service women (American- and foreign-born) choose to volunteer. It has been joked that three American women together naturally form themselves into a committee. They have a well-earned reputation around the world for their organizational skills. Social events and bazaars organized by the members of the American Women's Associations overseas would rival the efforts of the most highly paid event planners in the United States. It would be impossible to calculate the enormous sums of money they have raised for charities and the hours devoted freely to the work involved. Individuals also have contributed to projects that used their special qualifications and talents, thereby enhancing the image of the United States overseas. Foreign-born wives have contributed their skills to the volunteer effort, although for some of them it was a new experience.

Salote observed that volunteering in Fiji is viewed as an expatriate activity: "In Fijian culture, nobody volunteers except for people who are rich. Most people are either working or have too many things of their own to do at home. My first experience of volunteering was in Nigeria, and I found it very, very fulfilling. The women in the embassy in Lagos decided to do a fashion show to raise money for battered women. I was pregnant at the time, so I worked as a background person doing paperwork. We went out on the local economy and found a good designer, someone who was not so very successful that they wouldn't think of doing it, but someone who was kind of trying to get there. We found somebody and she designed the clothes. All the women in the embassy were the models. She also designed African outfits and did some summery beachwear and evening gowns. It was incredible. We actually helped establish her. She sold more than a hundred outfits just at the function that night. We printed tickets and sold them out in the expatriate community. Most of the embassy and oil people came. There was not much in terms of outings in Nigeria. People didn't have a chance to dress and go out on the town. We had a seven-course meal, and a lovely band in a big hotel. It was beautiful and we raised thousands of dollars."

Inger volunteered her nursing and administrative skills at several posts overseas, and especially recalls the years she spent in the Philippines and Sri Lanka. She said, "Through a close friend [in the Philippines], I became involved with the psychiatric hospitals, the leprosarium, and the homes for the handicapped she was establishing and running. She asked me to look after the orphanage because she was running so many different organizations. So I took over the Asilo De La Milabrosa, which had one hundred children, and ran it for four years. Before I left, I made sure that it could go on functioning without me. I put a trust fund in place so they can live off the interest forever, as long as they stay within the limit of one hundred children. It's still functioning well.

"My other project, apart from the orphanage, was Project Handclasp. Cebu is an island and a port and we had many American Navy ships coming in. My husband and I were always visiting and entertaining the crews, and I soon learned that the ships carried excess things from warehouses in the United States and were looking for places to donate them overseas. There could be anything from a ton of woolen sweaters to dishwashing powder, medicines, gauze, Band-Aids, or Q-tips. You never knew what was coming. They were always most interested in finding people they could trust to distribute the articles so they could reassure people back home that they went to needy places and not to the black market.

"I started writing the ships six to eight months in advance of when they would come out and asked them what they had. One time, we got a ton of potato salad. That's a lot of potato salad. I had the five-kilo cans stored in my friend's warehouse, and a couple of times a week I would open the cans from home, bring the girls from the house, and go down to the psychiatric hospital. People there were always hungry. Every piece of that one ton of potato salad was eaten by a needy person.

"Another time, they told me in advance that they had crutches. Would I be interested in crutches? I knew that there was a leprosarium about 25 kilometers north of Cebu. Leprosaria are villages, not just hospitals: villages where the relatives and children live with the patients. I contacted the Dutch nun who ran the place to see if she was interested, and she was. Because the ship was also carrying oil, it couldn't come all the way into port and we had to go out to it by helicopter. In order to travel in the helicopter, the nun had to remove her headgear, which she hadn't removed in public for fifty years. Initially, she couldn't do it, but finally she said, 'Never mind, the Lord will understand.' So she put on her earmuffs and off we went. We delivered the crutches and you just cannot believe the sight of hundreds of people who for years hadn't moved about, now mobile.

"Another time we had spare parts from a cardiac unit somewhere in California. I invited all the cardiologists in Cebu. They pawed through these like it was Christmas and found parts for their instruments that they had been lacking for years. All of these things were possible because of American goodwill."

Years later, when her husband was assigned to Sri Lanka as head of the Colombo Plan, Inger worked as a back-up nurse for the health unit at the American embassy. But she spent most of her time volunteering as the chairman of the board of a small hospital in Colombo, the Joseph Fraser Hospital. The Tamil insurrection was going on in the north and northeast of the island, and Sinhalese anarchists (known by their acronym JVP) were terrorizing the population in the south.

"The minister of defense, Lalith Athulayh Modali, had been very badly injured by a bomb in the parliament a year or so after we got there," she said. "He required very specialized medicine because his intestines had basically been blown apart. I went to the Agency people and asked if they could help me get the medicine for him through Singapore or Bangkok. They had it flown in and, I think because of that, Lalith survived that assassination attempt.

"Six months later, all the hospitals in Sri Lanka were declared closed by the JVP except my hospital. I could never quite figure out who was keeping a hand over me. I never dared to ask Lalith but in the back of my mind I thought he had something to do with it. We were the only hospital that functioned for six solid weeks in all of Sri Lanka with total warfare going on. We worked twenty-four hours. It was an assembly line until we were out of anesthesia and antibiotics, but we managed to stay open. Unfortunately, two years after we left, Lalith was killed by another assassin.

"I always felt that as long as I could be useful, and as long as I could do something in the local settings, I was very happy. It didn't matter that I was a volunteer. There are so many things that can be done all over the world, and particularly in the Third World countries. I realized I was lucky to have a medical background because I could fit in anywhere. Even if it was working for the local vet, anesthetizing cats and dogs for the first few months we were there before I got connected with a hospital. I think in a sense that's why I look back at our foreign service life as a very privileged lifestyle. I met so many sensational people."

Elisabeth Herz continued to volunteer her medical skills during her husband's subsequent postings to Tehran, Iran; and Saigon, South Vietnam. "Of all our postings, I loved Iran the best," she said. "The culture was fascinating to me. We were there from 1963 to 1967. Martin was the political counselor and then chargé for quite a while. We were invited everywhere and met many interesting people in and out of government. We traveled as widely as we could and often by car into the desert. I volunteered as a gynecologist/obstetrician at a hospital in Tehran, and through my work established my own contacts, including the minister of health and his wife. I worked on population control programs there, which were supported by Farah Diba, the wife of the Shah. (We provided educational programs, but one of the most effective things we did was to give the poor villagers battery-operated radios. These provided them with alternative entertainment in the evenings.)

"My medical contacts were a great help when we had a personal emergency. One hot Friday afternoon, we were entertaining some American and Iranian health officials at the swimming pool at our residence. My husband slipped on the wet surface surrounding the pool and fell and broke his hip. By the time we got him to the hospital, he was in shock. One of the Iranian doctors who had been at our house told us of an Iranian orthopedic surgeon who was American-trained and offered to try to get hold of him. Because it was Friday, this was unlikely, so I had everyone telephoning to line up transportation to fly Martin to Wiesbaden in

Germany. We also had to find the embassy security officer so that he would be present in the event the surgeon was found and Martin would be under anesthetic.

She continued, "The surgeon did come, but I was still very worried and spoke with him privately. I told him I was also a surgeon and that I wanted him to operate on the condition that I observed. If I did not think the surgery was going well, he would sew up and we would fly my husband out. I knew I had a nerve asking that of him, but it was my husband he was operating on. The surgeon agreed immediately, which showed me that he felt quite secure. He started to operate, and after a short time I could see that he knew what he was doing. He had to put a metal pin in the hip—probably not the most modern—but still it was well done."

From 1968 to 1970, Martin Herz was assigned to the American embassy in Saigon. At that time, only the wives of senior embassy officers were allowed to accompany their husbands there. His position was minister for political affairs, so Elisabeth was able to go. Conditions were dangerous, however, and everyone lived on a compound. Elisabeth had to be accompanied at all times and driven in an armored car.

Before leaving Washington, she volunteered for the American Medical Association (AMA) program working with the civilian population in Saigon. There was a very large ob/gyn hospital there, run by a Catholic doctor from North Vietnam who had moved south because of the war. He had refused assistance from the AMA program but, because she felt as an ob/gyn physician that she would be most useful there, Elisabeth went to see him. Again, Professor Antoine's name opened the door for her and she was welcomed.

Of the country's approximately six hundred doctors, only two hundred were working with the civilian population. Elisabeth was asked to spend her mornings training new doctors before she saw her ob/gyn patients in the afternoon. There was a lot of work to be done: "The first day the professor showed me around the hospital, we went to the labor room. There were so many women there I could not count them. They were lying across beds that had been pushed together. There was an eerie feeling about the place and I suddenly realized why. Women were giving birth without any sound or movement. I asked the professor what painkillers they were taking. He told me they took nothing, not even an aspirin. I observed this over and over again.

"Later, I had occasion to ask the wife of a government minister about it. She explained that because Vietnamese lived in such cramped conditions, any loud complaining would be intolerable for everyone, and they were taught from an early age not to show pain. Besides, childbirth was a happy event. She compared it to the difference between the Western and Eastern ways of mourning death, which is a sad event. Vietnamese cry out and comfort each other, while Americans are quiet and hide their grief.

She went on, "I was kept very busy. After their deliveries, many of the women had intestinal trouble, or severe anemia, tuberculosis—all kinds of problems—so we couldn't send them home right away. The wards were very crowded. Sometimes up to five women were lying across two beds and the babies would be on newspaper because there was no laundry facility.

"In Japan, Iran, and South Vietnam I was able to put my medical training to good use. When you are able to choose volunteer work, then you are doing something that is close to your heart for some reason. The most important thing is that you are engaged. I have had wonderful experiences overseas, which I would not have had if I had waited for someone to pay me."

Today, depending on the post, more employment opportunities are available to wives in the foreign service, and the decision to work or not is a personal one. The fact remains that frequent moves hinder long-term employment, and certain types of careers are impossible. Those women who can afford to and who enjoy volunteering continue to do so, and find their contributions needed and appreciated. Others choose not to work and welcome the opportunity to spend more time with their children. Raising children in the foreign service can be a job all by itself.

Chapter Five

Children: Language and Identity

Inger had her second child in Madagascar. There was no doctor or anesthesia, only a midwife who smoked a cigar throughout the labor. Anna's second child was born in Papua New Guinea. She had a bed in the high-cost ward ($12 a day) and the baby slept in a plastic cribette that resembled an old meat safe with mosquito netting. Some of the other women had their babies in Washington, D.C., with help at home from their mothers, who flew in for a few weeks or months. Others chose to go back to their countries to avail themselves of extended family help.

Maggy comes from Belgium. She was planning to have her first child in Washington where her husband was assigned, but their onward assignment to Indonesia was brought forward, which meant she would have been left in Washington to have the baby on her own. Arrangements agreed to by the State Department allowed her, seven weeks before her due date, to fly to Brussels, where she would stay with her mother while her husband went to post. When the birth was imminent, he would join her in Brussels. Then, when Maggy and the baby were cleared to travel, they would follow him to Indonesia. The logistics were complicated and Maggy arrived in Jakarta exhausted, wondering what she was getting herself into because the airline crews had kept asking her why she would take a newborn to post-coup Indonesia.

No matter where the children were actually born, the biggest concerns of the parents were how to raise them, in which language to speak to them, and how to give them a sense of cultural identity while moving them from place to place. The term "third culture kid" describes those children who create a third culture separate from their passport country (the country of their parents), where they spend little time, and the country or countries where they are raised. This third culture is made up of children who have similar experiences, not origins.[1] Children of marriages where the mother and father are from different countries, and who are raised in neither of those countries, have an added dimension to their experience.

On one of her trips to visit us in Virginia when my daughters were young, my mother remarked, somewhat wistfully, "The girls don't sound at all like you, do they." She was right: there wasn't a trace of Strine between them.[2] Their ears picked up what they heard around them in the classroom and playground, and they spoke American English. My accent was mine alone and my pronunciation of certain words even a source of amusement to them. It didn't bother me; it seemed natural that they would speak with the dominant accent of their community. About the only Australian things I can think of that I passed on to them are a taste for Vegemite in my older daughter and books about Blinky Bill, the koala, and Shy, the platypus. While my daughters seem to enjoy their Australian connection, they have never thought of themselves as anything but Americans with an Australian mother. The differences between Americans and Australians are subtle ones of attitude and worldview rather than of language and custom. We have not been assigned to Australia, and have only spent short vacations there. Had we stayed for extended periods, it might have been different. In the countries where we were assigned, the girls identified totally with the American community.

Anna, who is from New Zealand, found that her sons picked up some Down Under attitudes during the family's postings to New Zealand and Australia. She said, "My husband and I suspected that three years in Australia and then two years in New Zealand would put the children in a much more difficult position of readjustment when we returned to the U.S., and it has happened in exactly the way that we predicted. In the long run, I hope that we are not going to regret it. While there are not distinct racial, linguistic, and ethnic differences between the countries, we have children who are dual culture. They are not quite certain whether they are New Zealanders or Americans.

"It has come out in the college application process. American kids have learned that they've got to join all these clubs and have things to write about and say, 'See how great I am.' It's not seen here in the States as a negative to say, 'How great I am,' but the Australian and New Zealand way is not to push yourself forward. My sons are not comfortable with the American approach at all."

Chris is from England and when her son and daughter were young and the family was abroad at posts in Pakistan, Tunisia, Ghana, and Egypt, she sent or accompanied them to England to spend vacations in a family holiday house with cousins. Now adults, her children don't visit as often, and they consider themselves to be Americans. She said, "I find myself being slightly a figure of fun as far as the kids are concerned: 'Oh, Mum, you're so British.' My daughter, especially, I think, feels totally American. We sent her to boarding school in Virginia for her last two years of high school, and she went on to college in Massachusetts. She loves American sports. She plays touch football, she was always on the softball team, and she likes being American. She's now in the hotel and restaurant business. I don't think she would ever want to work abroad unless she was in the fold of some terribly American operation of some kind.

"My son also went to boarding school in the States for two years. During his junior year of college, we pushed him to have a year abroad in France. He enjoyed that very much and then came to stay with us in Bulgaria, where we were posted. He worked there on a contract and ended up staying four years. Being a foreigner was a status that he liked. That's not the case with my daughter at all. What she likes is being in charge and knowing everything about the place where she is."

For many of the women whose mother tongue is not English, passing their language on to their children was very important. The children of the younger women are still babies, so it remains to be seen how successful they will be. For the older ones, success depended a great deal on the personality of the child. In some cases, because the families moved so much, other languages got in the way. Serving in countries where their language was spoken reinforced the efforts of others. Experiences varied widely, but in almost every case, the husband spoke his wife's language and supported her wish to pass it along to the children.

Frederique expressed hopes that were common among the young mothers: "My son is only seventeen months old, but my goal is to raise him and all our following kids bilingual, French and English. As a linguist, I feel it's a huge advantage and a wonderful present I can give him. I wish I had had the chance to speak another language without an accent. My husband is very supportive of my teaching our son both the French language and culture, and this is very important. I want my children to feel they are half French as well as half American. I want them to feel the same strong attachment I have for my hometown, my family, the French culture and food."

Tanja, however, is having problems teaching Croatian and English to her two-year-old daughter. She said, "It's hard because she is confused. Most of her friends can now make little sentences, but she can't really. She's saying a few words now, but that's because a couple of weeks ago I decided to stop the Croatian thing. Not to stop it completely, but to do a little bit more of English at home. She's now picking up words and saying things, but it's frustrating for her and us. She can understand both languages. The pediatrician says to keep on trying and one day she will just do it. It's an important issue because my mother doesn't speak any English."

Didem's daughter is seven. "I always speak Turkish at home," she said. "My daughter understands everything. When she was two, we went to visit my family in Istanbul and she forgot English, picking up Turkish very fast. When we came back, she didn't speak English for a while. I remember telling her how cute I thought it was. This year when we went, thinking she was going to forget her English again, she refused to speak Turkish. Then just the other day, we were at the mall and I was speaking to her in Turkish and asking her things and she said, 'Please don't speak Turkish around here. Everybody speaks English.' I just looked at her. I was not expecting that. I would like her to speak Turkish so that she can talk with my mother, who doesn't speak any English. When my daughter was younger, and people asked her where she was from, she would answer: 'I am Turkish and my mom's Turkish too.' I don't think she would say that now; she would say she's American."

Lourdes, from Peru, has two children who grew up overseas, with only short visits to the United States on home leave. Lourdes has spoken to them in Spanish all their lives, and they are bilingual. "They don't have any accent, but my daughter has more fluency than my son," she said. "As a teenager, he resisted speaking Spanish; it was more a rebellion against me than the language. We had tours in Spain and Argentina so both of them spoke it outside the home. In Spain, I put my son in the Boy Scouts; in Argentina, I sent him one summer to a *stancia*, a goucho farm, which he just loved. There, he had to speak Spanish. In spite of the temporary resistance to speaking Spanish, he never really considered himself totally American. He's a real 'third culture kid.'

"We later moved to Vienna, Austria, where he had his last two years of high school. At a parent/teacher meeting, I chatted with his chemistry teacher. She said she would have liked to pair my son in the lab with another American student, but he was the only one, so she paired him with a Scandinavian. When I told my son about there being only one American in the class, he said, 'Who's the American?' I said, 'You!' He said, 'Oh, right.' Both my son and daughter returned to Virginia for college, where they studied electrical engineering. They are now married to Americans and living in the United States."

Both Maggy's sons are graduates of the U.S. Naval Academy. They are fluent French speakers, but not because she forced it on them. She said, "It was more circumstances to start with. I made a decision with the first baby. When we were in Indonesia, I realized that other kids turned to look at me when I spoke French. I thought, 'Oh my gosh, I can't do this to my child,' and so I spoke English. Also, people who had experienced this advised me not to speak three languages with the child because it would confuse him and he would speak nothing properly. So I thought, 'OK. Indonesian I cannot avoid because we were speaking it every day in the house with the help. English I will never avoid, of course, so I will just drop French,' which I did. So my son spoke Indonesian and English. Then we went to Malaysia and this sort of continued: local language and English. Then to Kuwait—Montessori and the British School. From Kuwait we went to Palermo in Italy, where he went to school in Italian, total immersion in Italian. English at home all through.

"During our Palermo posting, I went for an extended stay in Brussels for medical reasons. I took the two boys with me. (The second one, who was born in Malaysia, was in nursery school at this point.) It was still the school year, so my brother-in-law, who is a teacher, took the two boys into his school. Because they both had Italian, within two weeks they could communicate in French. By the time I had recuperated from my surgery, my husband had received official notification that we were to be assigned to Brussels, so I went back to Palermo to pack out and we returned to Belgium.

"The older son was going into the second grade. At this point, we started panicking, thinking it was time we put him into an American school. The embassy people were supposed to send their children to the Department of Defense (DOD) school in Brussels, so we sent the older one there. We chose to put the younger boy into a Belgian kindergarten and then left him in the same school because we were not particularly happy with the DOD school. He went to nursery, kindergarten, first and second grades all in French. He learnt all his multiplication tables in French, everything. He was totally bilingual. The older one was in the American school, so I put him in the Belgian Boy Scouts so he would have the opportunity to speak French too. So that's how they both became bilingual: the younger one in his school and the older through three years in the Belgian Boy Scouts. After that, I spoke French with them at home. They continued to study it in school and they were both president of the French Club at the Naval Academy. So it served them well."

Muriel, also from Belgium, did not start out speaking French with her son and daughter. She said, "We spoke French in the house when we were assigned to Algeria because the maid only spoke that or Arabic, but my son was young then. Later, when we were going to Central Africa, I started trying to speak to both children in French. My son was very embarrassed. He said, 'Why are you speaking this funny language? I don't need it.' I said, 'Well, maybe not now, but once we get to Bangui you will find a different story. You are going to a French school because there is nothing else.' So, came the first day of school and I dropped him off and hoped for the best. Of course, he was not the only foreign child, but he was very young—in the second grade—and I didn't feel very happy about the whole thing. But you sink or swim. Within six months he was speaking fluently with his friends. My daughter went to kindergarten, but she found an American friend there and French took second place."

Maria Bauer grew up in Prague and left at the beginning of World War II. "My mother made a special effort to have us educated in the other languages," she said. "English was my fourth language. I never went to German school, but I spoke German always at home with my parents. I spoke Czech with my friends. I did my baccalaureate in French, which was like a second language. I spoke German to my husband, but in front of our son and daughter we always spoke English. I would not teach them German. I had my resentment. I felt German was finished after the war, that nobody would speak it. I thought French would be the language. So I tried to teach my children French. I had a group of American children I taught French to so that my daughter would join, but she was so impossible in class that I kicked her out. Then I was stuck teaching all the other children!

"But it wasn't only resentment against Germany: I wanted my children always to be at home. I knew some refugees who came over and the children had a German accent or a Czech accent and other children made fun of them. So I decided my children would be Americans from the start, and I succeeded. My daughter became a real American teenager and later they both married Americans.

"My son was happy in the foreign service and adjusted anywhere. He spoke fluent Arabic and he also did very well in school. Later, when he went to university and studied history, he was furious with me. 'Why didn't you teach me German?' he wanted to know. So then I tried to teach him when I had time, because he became interested in his background."

Annabella is from Guatemala and although she speaks fluent English, she insists that her son and daughter, who are in high school, speak Spanish with her. "I think it is a shame to have the opportunity to speak another language and not take it," she said. "I spoke to my children in Spanish from the beginning. We were in Belize when they were little, so Spanish is their first language. My son then went to a British school there and had some problems because his English was not that good. When we came to the States he had to go to English as a Second Language (ESL) classes. He lasted six months, got bored, and refused to go any more. The principal let him go to regular classes and go to ESL for just a couple of hours. At this point, my husband and I started to speak English with the children at home to reinforce it. When they were older and their English was good, I switched back to Spanish.

"There was a stage when they didn't want to speak Spanish because they felt different. They wanted to show that they also could speak English. Then when we moved to Ecuador, it was different: English in school and everything outside in Spanish. Now they are teenagers and are at a stage where they are proud that they know the other language. My son especially. In the United States, when we are in a store I speak English with them and then my son refuses to speak. He asks me, 'Why do you speak English? This is our language.' He feels pride that part of him is Guatemalan. He wants to take the SAT [Scholastic Aptitude Test] in Spanish. Even though the only time he took Spanish classes was in Ecuador, his Spanish is very good, including the vocabulary. My daughter I have to remind to speak in Spanish, although she understands everything and sometimes even corrects my husband. When she speaks to me in

English, I reply in Spanish. Why should you lose a language when you have it at home?"

Michele wanted her children to be 100 percent American, but with a love of France and the language, and the capacity to go to France and feel "I'm an American, but I'm at ease here." She said she succeeded in raising them to be completely American, but the language was a problem, especially with her daughter.

She said, "In 1967, we were evacuated from Yemen because of the Six Day War in Israel. I took the children, who were four and three years old, and stayed with my family in Paris. Our son was slow in speaking. In the house in Yemen, I was speaking French to him; my husband and I were speaking English to each other; my husband was speaking English to the children; and we spoke to the servants in Arabic. While we were in Paris, both children started to speak French like everyone around them, and by the time my husband came six months later, I had two children who spoke nothing but French and had completely forgotten their English.

"Then we were posted to Libya and our daughter was ready for kindergarten. The one good one there was British-run. She couldn't communicate with anybody at school because at that point she could speak only French. The night of her second day there, she started having nightmares: 'No, Mummy, you are not French. No, Mummy, you are not French.' It lasted about two or three weeks, not wanting to go to school, temper tantrums. Finally, I went to the doctor and said, 'What am I going to do? This child has nightmares every night. She doesn't even wake up.' He said, 'Drop the French.' I said, 'I don't want to do that.' 'Drop it now.' So I did. I told my daughter that we would speak English. Mummy was French, but it was not going to interfere with our life from now on. My daughter had the first good night's sleep in three weeks.

"But we had created a problem: mother was now communicating in English with the children, and how to go back on it. The battle for the language continued. When our daughter was in sixth and seventh grade, I got her the same courses I had taken in school. She did the American curriculum and her homework plus half the program a French child would have. So in two years she had one year of the French school."

Inger says that her teaching Danish to her son and daughter came quite naturally. They are now adults and still speak to her in Danish and to their father in English. "Primarily, my reasoning was that it was the only way I could give them a natural insight into half their culture. After all, they are half Danish and will always be half Danish. If I didn't do it through the language, how could I do it? Besides, I didn't know any nice nursery rhymes, or songs, or stories in English. I only knew them in Danish. It was quite natural for me to speak to them in Danish from the day they were born. I have never had resentment from the children. Even when they've had friends over, or in company with other people, they have always responded to me in Danish. When we are sitting at the dining table at night, it's boom, boom, boom, both ways back and forth and always has been: Danish to me and English to my husband. He is also fluent in Danish, so it is not as if I am having a side conversation with the kids that he can't understand. But my mother and her siblings in Denmark didn't speak a word of English. Had I not from the very beginning taught my children Danish, they would have had no communication with my elder relatives. When my son and daughter became old enough to understand, they both expressed appreciation that I did that with them, and that was a nice feeling.

"When we lived in Sri Lanka, we sent the children to summer school in Denmark every year, and that was very fruitful because there they were with many other kids with one parent being Danish. Later, they both went to Denmark for a year of university."

In Soon did not force her children to speak Korean, although they did pick up a little. When the family was assigned to Japan, her daughter went to a Japanese playgroup and spoke like a Japanese child. When they left the country, she forgot most of her Japanese, but she later studied it in college and, according to In Soon, her Japanese is now very good. After graduating from college, she chose to go to Japan to teach English. Both children are interested in their Korean backgrounds but consider themselves to be Americans. In Soon said, "Maybe they look different than a Caucasian boy and girl, but their thinking is American. I am 50 percent in them, but I sometimes wonder where that 50 percent went. Their thinking and behaving is not my way."

Bo-Yeon's daughter is nineteen, a student at the U.S. Air Force Academy, and her son is seventeen and in high school. They are bilingual, speaking Korean with her and English with their father. Bo-Yeon said, "My husband was assigned to Indonesia just after our daughter, was born. While he was getting settled there, I took the baby and went to Korea to stay with my parents for a month. At first, my mother seemed uncomfortable with the baby and spoke a sort of 'Konglish' to her. I said, 'Why don't you play with her and sing and talk to her like a Korean child? Speak to her in Korean.' So she did, and my daughter responded to the Korean sounds. From then on, I spoke to her in Korean too. I did the same with my son, who was born in Singapore during the Indonesian tour."

She added, "My son and daughter are both tall and their facial features are a mix of Caucasian and Korean. When my daughter was about three, and we were in Seoul on a visit, she asked me why her eyes looked different from her cousins' eyes. I explained that she was a mixture, but that it was a good thing, because she could enjoy kimchi as well as hamburger. She liked that idea. I think both our children feel they have the advantages of both cultures, and feel comfortable with friends from either background. Although, my son lately seems to have mostly Asian friends."

Hala believes that she set aside much of her culture in order for her daughter, an only child, to have a secure American identity. "I feel that when you have kids in a cross-cultural marriage in the foreign service, you also have to worry about making them feel they belong somewhere," she said. "And it's even more challenging because you've got that other culture and you're living in several other cultures. I made a decision early on when I realized how confused my daughter was about being a foreign service kid. When we were living in Oman, she thought she was Omani. I wanted her to feel she belonged somewhere, and if that somewhere had to be America (because Lebanon was really up in flames, and I didn't think that was going to be an option anyway), then I really worked hard to come back to the United States every couple of years. We put her in a private school in Washington and she went back to it when we were assigned to Washington, and it was the best thing we ever did. She's very grounded as an American, but it's because she is so grounded and comfortable being an American that she's now free to explore her Lebanese/Arab identity.

"When she was tiny, I used to speak to her in Arabic and French and English, and she rebelled. She didn't want me to speak Arabic to her, so I didn't. But I paid a price. By not teaching her my language, everything that comes with the language I couldn't teach her either. There are things in your native language that you can't translate. Looking back, it was a sad moment to decide not to teach her, but it was important for her feelings of security. But I'm so happy she has decided, at twenty-four, that she wants to learn it and to speak it, because it is part of who she is."

Wati has a son in college and a daughter in middle school. "When they were babies I spoke to them in English," she said. "I also tried to teach them Indonesian but I didn't really follow it through. When we visited Indonesia they learned fast, but when we came back to the States they didn't want to speak it because they didn't want to be different. They even told me, 'Mummy, speak American to us. Don't speak Indonesian.' I still remember my son saying that to me when he was only little. But when they didn't want people to know what they were saying, they would speak Indonesian like a secret code."

Even though the women accepted that their children would have an American identity, many of them wanted their own cultural values to be incorporated into their upbringing. Some found that their American husbands had much more liberal ideas about raising children than they did.

Michele said, "A lot of the time in the foreign service, you are father and mother because your husband is gone so much. I went to the extent of being much too disciplined because he was much too lax when he was home. For him, it was easy to just say yes. I remember dragging him one day to the bathroom and saying, 'You do not say yes behind my back. You first say, What did your mother say? Whatever she said I stand by.' I gave in a bit over the years, but I was trying to impose the strict discipline that my father had.

"To this day my children remind me that they shocked their friends when they told them that I watched television with them. I was so appalled at the content of American television. When they were allowed to watch an hour of television, I watched the program with them. And when an advertisement came on, I would say, 'Oh don't believe that. What a nice actor he is, telling you to buy such and such.' I would burst all the bubbles. I told them I would never buy them anything if they said they had seen it on television.

"When my husband and I made our wills, I insisted that if anything happened to the two of us, my parents would take the children. I was quite happy to have them raised as Americans, but to be brought up by somebody else without the influence of the French side, oh no."

Helga and her husband decided to raise their two sons as Americans, with a German background. They have had a couple of assignments in Germany. She said, "The older one says he's half-German, but they don't like to speak German as much as English because it's not as easy and they don't know it as well. But they speak it with my brother and sister, and they used to with my parents when they were alive. They watch German kids TV without any problem, laugh at the jokes, and say German things here and there. For a while, the older one didn't want to speak German at all, and I forced him. We had a big disagreement but now he loves German school and he has a wonderful teacher. But I want them to know that America is the center of their life and that is where they will go to college. I would like them to be able to say, 'I know more than the average American because I speak German, and I understand Germany better than the average American because I have a German mother.'"

In Soon said she feels she was unsuccessful in imparting traditional Korean family values to her children. "American fathers are much more liberal and give the children more freedom. I cannot do that because of the way I was brought up. Things like, girls should not go out with boys without their parents' permission. I tried to do things my own way, but I did not succeed."

Hala believed that the so-called American Protestant work ethic got in the way of her husband's spending enough time with their daughter. She said, "He would be at the embassy until seven o'clock at night and then we would go out to dinner at eight o'clock. I finally said, 'Wait a minute, I don't want to live like that!' He said, 'Well, this is the way it is. My father went to work at seven in the morning and came back at seven at night.' 'Well, my father came home in the middle of the day, we had a nice long lunch, a siesta, then I went back to school and he went back to work and somehow we all survived. You have to be home in time to be with our child.'

"It's also very hard for a lot of spouses to hand their children over to a nanny or a maid. I struggled with that in Kuwait when my daughter was small, because every maid I had there wanted to take over: 'Oh, madam, you go to your coffee.' 'No, madam is not going to her coffee, madam is staying home.' In Oman, where my husband was working hard, with a cocktail party every evening, I decided that I was not going to go to any more cocktail parties. That was bedtime-story time. I would go to dinners after eight-thirty. I said, 'Five or six years from now, will anybody really remember or care if I go or not? My daughter will remember I wasn't there for her, and that's my priority.' My husband agreed with me on this issue and said, fine."

Wati added that "there are times when I give my opinion about the appropriate way of behaving, such as making sure parents are home when my son is visiting his friends. He will say I am too conservative, that we are in America, not Indonesia. I say, 'It's not American or Indonesian. It's the way I would like you to behave and that's the rule in this family.' But he will say it's because I am Indonesian that I feel this way."

Salote has a nine-year-old son and a seven-year-old daughter. Traditional Fijian family customs would have been hard to enforce outside Fiji. She said, "When I was growing up, one of the most difficult traditions was that brothers did not speak directly to their sisters and sisters did not speak directly to their brothers. You had to go through your parents. You would never go close to your brothers, never sit near them. It was something you grew up with and you just accepted it. It has changed a lot now.

"My children feel as comfortable with my family as they do with their American relations. Fiji has been a transit point for us on our travels. We would spend some time there before moving on to somewhere else. Plus, every year my husband would pay for me to go back to Fiji with one or both of the kids. Now that we have had an assignment and lived for a longer period in Fiji, they know our house is there, and our house is here, and they feel very comfortable with that. They don't speak much Fijian. I had encouraged my nieces and nephews to speak it to them, so when they were playing they would start out speaking in Fijian. But at the back of their minds, they knew that my two are not Fijian speakers and they would switch to English, which they learn in school."

Faye Barnes's husband says, "I'm the only gringo in this family: my wife was born in Canada; one daughter was born in Venezuela; the other daughter in Peru; and the dog's Mexican." Faye regards her two daughters as "consummate foreign service children—they don't feel American or Canadian." Born overseas, they attended schools in Spain, Germany, Peru (and the younger one also in Mexico), and in Virginia. Both attended colleges in the United States. The older daughter spent her junior year abroad in Austria, and the younger daughter in England and Spain.

The older daughter finished college and accompanied her parents on assignment to London. She was no longer on their orders, but the British gave permission for her to work because, there, children are considered to be dependent until they are twenty-five. For a year, she worked off and on and took Christie's art history diploma. Then she moved to Guadelajara in Mexico and studied for a year for a Mexican art history diploma. She was then accepted into Tulane's Latin American studies master's program, but didn't like New Orleans, so returned to London where, through friends, she learned of a museum studies program at the University of East Anglia to which she was accepted. Said Faye, "Both girls are more comfortable in an international community, not in middle America. They have little in common with their cousins in Canada or the United States."

Many foreign service children have problems fitting in when they return to the United States for high school or college. Having spent many years outside the country, they have been influenced by other cultures rather than being shaped by a totally American experience. Because they have been moved often, some feel rootless. Others have enjoyed their school experiences abroad with an international group of students who understand what it's like to be the new kid in school. Some find it hard to settle into college, especially if their parents are assigned abroad and they are left behind, able to visit them at post only twice a year.

Foreign service children whose mothers are foreign-born appear to have experiences of foreign service life similar to those of children whose parents are both American-born, and the same problems at reentry. Most of them identify strongly with the United States in spite of only sporadic American experiences. At any age, whether in elementary or high school, they want to fit in.

At most overseas posts, there is an American or international school which provides English-language instruction leading to an American high school diploma or an international baccalaureate degree. These schools reflect the flavor of the countries in which they are located, but the student body is international. The majority of the older children of the women I interviewed came back to the United States for college and all ended up settling here, but many continue to be interested in travel and other cultures.

Annabella observed that her son and daughter "seem to look for their friends at school in the United States among kids who have also lived overseas and have had the same experiences so they can relate to them. Their friends are from the Philippines and Thailand. It's what they are used to. In Bucharest, Romania, our last post, my son's classroom had sixteen kids and only three were Americans. My son likes the idea of going to college in the United States but his idea for the future is to go overseas. He would like to live in Europe and is studying French. What interests him is knowing different cultures and languages, and getting to know new places."

Michele remembered that, "when we came back to the States from Libya, we didn't have much money and my parents bought a lot of the children's clothing. The first day our son went to nursery school, he came home in tears saying, 'I don't want to wear these clothes. People ask me why do I wear a bathing suit?' I had to go and buy some American clothing quickly.

"Years later, when we came back from another post and our daughter was in the tenth grade, she had a hard time making American friends. Her friends were Pakistani, Bangladeshi, you name it. Any nationality but American. She felt very rejected by the American kids, and she rejected them. My son had a different attitude. He came back in the ninth grade. I don't think he consciously said it, but he thought, 'I haven't had much sport in my life, so I'm going to join a team.' He tried everything. Everything. He came home one day and said, 'I can see that those guys with those jerseys with numbers on their chests are accepted by everybody. I'm going to get one of those.' He started lifting weights—this is a skinny guy—and then he got on to the football team.

"When we talked about school, he said that he had friends but that he didn't feel very close to them. He had very little in common with them. The first day of the semester, he said he was trying to explain to people where he had lived and they weren't interested. Instead, they were shocked that he didn't know the names of the football players or the baseball players. But he didn't reject. My daughter rejected and continued to have a very difficult time."

When Inger and her family returned to settle in Washington, her daughter was in high school and her son was entering his college freshman year. They reacted very differently from each other. She said, "The first day my daughter went to school, she dressed the way she would do in Sri Lanka, sort of European style. The next day she went to school, I couldn't recognize her. It was like a chameleon. I said, 'What happened?' 'I've got to fit in, Mom.' And that was the key word. And she did fit in. My son really had problems. He dropped out of college after a year and simply couldn't find his bearings. He was in and out of very different things. Then he went to Denmark to go to university for a year. When he came back, he said, 'I need the discipline. I'm going to join the U.S. Navy.' We said, 'Fine. Go for it.' He's very happy. He does photography in the Navy and he's advancing and very proud of himself."

For the children whose mothers are not Caucasian, their physical appearance is a sign of otherness, as it is for their mothers. They are much more likely to be asked about their backgrounds than are the children of mothers who are European in appearance, whose differences are internal and can be divulged, or not, according to the wishes of the child.

Salote said, "My son is quiet about what he feels. He'll say, 'My father is American.' But my daughter will say, 'I am half-Fijian because of my mother, and I am half-American because of my father.' She has no hesitation in telling everybody that."

Wati said, "I often ask my children how they feel, if they are treated differently, and they say no, they have no problems. My son they don't ask because maybe he looks more American. My daughter often gets questions about where she is from. Her features are more Asian than my son's."

Howard Kavaler said his daughters do not view themselves as Indians, but "they do love Indian food, and when I take them to an Indian restaurant, the little one will drink a mango lassi because her mother used to drink it. They can't understand why their friends don't like it as well. But neither has any experience of India."

His older daughter, who closely resembles Prabhi, was admitted to two private schools in Washington and couldn't choose between them. From one, she received an invitation to a reception for students and parents "of color." Howard said, "My daughter was really taken aback because she didn't understand why everyone wasn't invited to the reception. That decided for her; she chose the other school."

I did not interview any of the children—a separate study would be needed to gather their side of the discussion—but it appears that, for them, the mother's culture and language are an "extra," an added dimension. While they don't consider themselves to be "typical" Americans, they do identify themselves as Americans. What seems to be the best that a mother can hope for is the goal expressed by Michele: that the child be secure in his or her American identity, but have respect for and be comfortable with the mother's language and culture. The husband's positive attitude is important for this to be successful.

Sangeeta's Story

International from Birth

Sangeeta, now in her thirties, was born in Osaka and grew up in Kobe, Japan. Her mother is Japanese; her father was Indian. Until 1985, Japanese women could not pass their citizenship on to their children, so Sangeeta carried an Indian passport. She visited India for the first time when she was seventeen, and then returned when her father died in 1995 and the family gathered to scatter his ashes in the Ganges.

"I felt more Japanese because I was raised there and I speak the language, but I was not allowed Japanese citizenship or passport. When the law changed, I was over the age limit. My father was a textile importer. There were people from many different countries in Kobe, including about three hundred Indian families, most of them engaged in import/export businesses. My parents sent me to one of the five international schools in Kobe where most of the children were like me: part Japanese and part something else. By first grade I was speaking English and Japanese. My mother made sure that we spoke standard Japanese at home and we could also speak the Kobe and Osaka dialects. But I became English-dominant. I can read a Japanese newspaper, but I still have trouble writing. I never learned to write in Japanese beyond elementary school level.

"I lived in Japan until I was seventeen, when I went away to college, to Georgetown University in Washington, D.C. I met my husband there in my junior year, a year ahead of him. When I graduated, I worked for two years for a Japanese securities firm in Tokyo. After he graduated, he applied to the foreign service and, while waiting for his security clearances to be finalized, he traveled in Europe and then came to Tokyo where, for six months, he taught English and studied Japanese. We were married in Kobe in 1985 and moved to the Philippines, where he had been posted."

Chapter Six

Senior Wives

Just when foreign service officers are reaching their career goals of senior positions and increased responsibilities, many of their wives are tiring of the life. Children start college and must be left behind when the parents move overseas, their own parents are aging and require more attention, or the women feel that as their children grow older they have gained an opportunity to explore their own interests more fully.

The demands on the wives of ambassadors and deputy chiefs of mission are heavy. On paper, the wives have no rank or responsibilities, but in practice, a great deal is expected of them by the embassy community, the international diplomatic community, and the officials of the host government. More and more, one hears of senior officers' wives[1] deciding not to go to post at all, to visit periodically, or to go but limit their participation in official events.

In this matter, as in others, the foreign-born wives of senior officers I spoke to are in agreement with the American-born wives. Some of them have spent years supporting their husbands in their representational activities. Most of the foreign-born senior wives believed that home entertaining was important, even if they found it a burden. Their concerns were similar to those of the American-born wives in that they wouldn't mind the work so much if they were at least thanked by someone other than their husbands for doing it.

While in many cultures business entertaining is done in restaurants and hotels, the American way is to invite people home, especially when spouses are included. I recall how much our Chinese guests enjoyed visiting with our small daughters before dinner at our house in New Delhi, India. Chinese diplomats were required to leave their own children back home in China when assigned overseas, and they obviously missed them.

Chinese diplomats entertained us in their official embassy dining room at meals prepared by embassy chefs.

The U.S. government historically has taken home entertaining into account when allotting money for housing budgets overseas. Those officers with representational responsibilities were provided with living quarters large enough to accommodate a crowd, if necessary. Decreasing budgets and the square footage rule[2] have changed this somewhat, but American foreign service officers are still more likely to entertain an official contact at home than at a restaurant. Another reason for doing this (besides cultural) is that it is cheaper. The food and drink are covered by the office representational budget but the labor is free.

At one time or another, all wives have been asked to cook for, serve at, and otherwise create social functions that contribute to their husbands' work. Some women are good at it and enjoy it; some have no training for it and find it stressful; some can do it but would rather not. Others hate it and, if they can get away with it, refuse to do it. They find it time-consuming and at times demeaning, especially if the function is all male and they are required to cook and serve but are not asked to participate. Of all the ways in which wives have traditionally contributed to the work of the United States abroad, representational entertaining, for which they are paid nothing to perform, is the one that is the most contentious. It is also the area where senior wives find themselves spending increasing amounts of time, whether doing the work themselves or supervising a staff, and which, according to the AAFSW survey previously mentioned, causes them the most distress.

Anna entertained for her husband when he held senior positions in Papua New Guinea, Turkey, Australia, and New Zealand. She said, "I'm not an expert at giving parties, but I can do it. I think social contact, with spouses included, is an important part of the foreign service of any country. But you can't do it if you have a full-time job unless you have a full-time staff. If you're doing it yourself, it's a day or two for every party. This is not 'cocktails, cookies, and play,' this is work, and I have given too many hours gratis to the government over the years. In New Guinea we had heavy entertaining responsibilities and lots of visitors. We didn't have a cook and there wasn't enough money in the budget for caterers, so I had to do it all myself."

Hala said that, in her experience, "the role of the senior spouse is almost a full-time job, and there's never a word of thanks, except from your husband. As far as the State Department is concerned, you don't exist. But not only that, when *you* need something, they treat you like a problem, a liability rather than an asset. For example: the last time I went to the training seminar for the spouses of principal officers, an employee from the Department came in and proceeded to say, 'Well, you've got to have a separate kitchen for your stuff. Make sure you don't mix the flour for the entertainment with the flour you use for your own food, or the sugar.' All the wives were sitting there very nicely, and I just blew up. I was so angry. I said, 'Wait a minute. How dare you say such a thing! We are free slave labor for the State Department, and you are going to nickel-and-dime us for a cup of flour and a cup of sugar! Not in your life. I will never keep a separate kitchen. And I don't care if the inspectors come. You go back and tell them that this is not acceptable!' I was livid. And then all the other women erupted. So we had a mini-revolution and the woman from the Department was speechless.

"Once, when my daughter and I were evacuated out of Oman, I had no access to anything. We had to keep sending messages back to my husband and say, 'Oh, we need you to send a message to say that it's OK for me to cash this check, it's OK for me to get into storage.' I think it was just the beginning of FLO and I didn't even know it existed. I was angry that we were treated with so much suspicion. Little things started to really get to me and sometimes I would think, 'Is that because I'm foreign-born, or just because I'm a spouse?' Things like entering the sacrosanct, the embassy, and having to be escorted. Well, I'm the consul-general's wife, dammit! What do you expect me to do? It's just so humiliating. And really, as far as I'm concerned, the foreign service treats spouses very, very poorly.

"At our last post, Saudi Arabia, my husband was consul-general. I really thought hard about whether I wanted to go or not. I was so tired of going overseas, and one of my conditions was that if I couldn't work, do my art therapy, I wasn't staying. I just was not willing to do the social scene and the tea parties and the dinner parties. Fortunately, it turned out that I was able to work as an art therapist there. I was very busy and got to know a lot of Saudis. Because of the local conditions, and being the consul-general's wife, I couldn't just go out and open up a clinic, so I had a private practice working out of our house, in relationship to a center. So I was very busy. My work was full time and I did the social stuff only as much as I wanted to. I had a good household staff, I trained them well, and basically I didn't have to be there for my husband to be able to do his entertaining. I only went to the things I wanted to go to, and if people didn't like it, that was just tough. If it was interesting or too much of an affront not to go, I went, but in general I tried to chart my own way."

Anna Maria's husband held senior positions in Guatemala and Brazil. In Guatemala, in particular, she remembers being extremely busy with fundraising activities and entertaining. Both she and her husband were fluent in Spanish so were able to have a wide circle of acquaintances outside the embassy. She said, "My husband always said that I wasn't forced to do anything, I could do as I pleased, but we always entertained beyond the expectations of the job because we enjoyed meeting people. I made friends with people who remain friends today, even after I am no longer involved in the foreign service."

Sangeeta's husband was principal officer at the American consulate in Nagoya, Japan, for three years. She said, "Nagoya is really provincial compared to Kobe and Tokyo. I joined two international women's groups. One of them only had sixteen foreigners and a hundred Japanese so we were in a more Japanese context. I was talked into being on the board and was very busy with the club-related activities. They all saw me as a bridge between the expatriate wives and the Japanese members because I could speak both languages. They did not think of me as Japanese: I was the

American consul's wife who happened to be half Japanese. On the one hand, that "exalted" position had certain rules of behavior attached to it, but I was young compared to the senior Japanese ladies who were the wives of local doctors and lawyers. The spouses of my husband's Japanese counterparts were also older.

"In Japan it's hard to get household help, and I had to train somebody to help me with the entertaining. A lot of social events were men only. There were occasions when we hosted at our home, which was an official residence, and I was the only woman present. I would usually stay, because most of the Japanese men were familiar with American ways and would try to include me in the conversations."

Depending on the country of assignment, the wife of an ambassador or consul-general can be involved in a lot more than entertaining in the official residence. In some countries, she has a very high profile and is expected to support the local women's organization and lend her name and her time to other charitable pursuits. Some women have been able to use their position as wife of the senior American representative in a country to make significant contributions.

One such wife was among the recipients of the AAFSW/Secretary of State's Award for Outstanding Volunteerism Abroad in 2000.[3] Lynne Montgomery is the British-born wife of the U.S. ambassador to Croatia from 1998 to 2000. I did not interview her; the following is a condensed version of the citation published by the AAFSW describing her wide-ranging accomplishments in Croatia:

The four-year war for independence in Croatia that ended in 1995 resulted in physical and psychological trauma. As the wife of the American ambassador, Lynne was in a unique position to capture the attention of the media to create awareness of the need that existed in Croatia. She focused her efforts on fostering volunteerism in three main areas: the de-mining of Croatia; improvements in the healthcare sector; and production of multi-cultural events as fundraisers to support over 20 charities aimed at aiding victims of war trauma.

After visiting war-torn areas, she convinced the Croatian Mining Center (CROMAC), the organization responsible for managing de-mining, to join her in a fundraising campaign to expand the de-mining efforts. She approached the American Chamber of Commerce (AMCHAM) in Croatia and suggested a plan to engage their members in an "adopt a minefield" campaign. She worked tirelessly with CROMAC and AMCHAM securing commitments from members and matching funds from the Slovenian Trust fund for approximately $100,000. At Lynne's request, the director of partnership programs at the U.S. Department of State brought a delegation from the U.S. to Croatia. After meeting with school children unable to play in the fields, widows whose husbands were killed trying to grow food for their families, and politicians desperate to rebuild the economies of their small towns, additional pledges for over $350,000 for de-mining projects were secured. A group of vintners from California, Roots for Peace, are exploring the possibility of de-mining former vineyards and investing in expansion of the Croatian wine industry. Lynne will be hosting a delegation representing several major U.S. vineyards. Her de-mining efforts have been so successful that the wife of the prime minister of Croatia is joining forces with her to demonstrate the new Croatian government's concern for the issue. In addition to this work, Lynne also

- *started a drama club for children and worked on a joint production between American and Croatian children. With Croatian actors and actresses she produced two Shakespearean plays, performed a dozen times in multiple cities in Croatia raising more than $20,000;*
- *worked closely with medical professionals to organize a conference on spouse and child abuse, recruiting specialists from Croatia and the United States and other countries;*
- *recruited and raised funds for a team of psychiatric counselors to work with exhumation teams at mass graves; and*
- *initiated a project to renovate drab wards into more cheerful environments for terminally ill children at a hospital in Zagreb.*

By any measure, this is an extraordinary list of achievements. In other places, this type of involvement is impossible.

Elisabeth Herz accompanied her husband to Sofia when he was appointed ambassador to Bulgaria by President Ford in 1974. The three-year assignment was extremely interesting for him,[4] but for Elisabeth it was less than enjoyable. The embassy was small and in a hostile environment, the residence was bugged, the phones were tapped, and the servants were trained and supplied by the KGB.

"I felt like I was in a golden cage," she said. "I tried to do a few social things with the other women in the embassy, but I think all of us were finding it very difficult. When we wanted to invite Bulgarians to functions at the embassy, we had to submit their names to the foreign ministry for approval. We had some parties where there were more waiters than guests. Because the hotels were poor, everybody who came stayed with us at the residence. I became a glorified hotelkeeper and guide.

"For myself, there were several reasons the tour was an unhappy one. The first was that I was not permitted to practice medicine, even as a volunteer. I asked the ministry if I could at least get to know some doctors, walk the rounds with them, and exchange experiences, but I was told that it was impossible. (I had some medical problems while were in Bulgaria, but I was flown out to Wiesbaden and Vienna for treatment.) The second was that living again in a dictatorship was for me very unpleasant. It brought back memories of the Nazi times in Austria. The whole atmosphere was very depressing. The third reason was a very nasty experience I had near the beginning of our time in Sofia."

She recalled, "My mother had come from Vienna to visit. It was very hot in Sofia, so I decided to take her to spend a few days in the embassy dacha, which was in a lovely wooded area outside a small village. On the last day, we went for a walk in the forest. Along the trail, I saw a typical Bulgarian workman walking towards us. He stopped and asked us who we were. In the little Bulgarian I knew, I told him that we were foreigners visiting the country. He stretched out his hand to shake mine and the moment he held my hand, he threw me to the ground and tried to rape me. My mother, who was very frail, attacked him from behind with her walking stick. He was distracted by this long enough for me to get free and I ran shouting for help. He ran after me and attacked me again. By this time we were close to a house and I was screaming loudly, so he eventually gave up and ran off. My clothes and shoes were torn and I practically carried my mother to the nearby house.

"There were two Bulgarian men there and one of them spoke a little English. I asked him to call the embassy. He tried, but said he could not get through, so I asked him to help us get back to our dacha, which he did. From there, I had him call the police and ask them to call the embassy. The next morning my husband came and took us back to Sofia.

"When my husband reported the attack to the foreign ministry, they said it was all my imagination and that something like that couldn't happen in Bulgaria. I was extremely angry and insisted that they send a doctor to examine my mother and me and make a report. I was covered in bruises from the man's hands and from being thrown on the ground. My mother was also bruised because he had thrown her down, as well. Eventually, they agreed to send a doctor and he did make a report. After some time, we heard they had arrested somebody who had been released from jail around the time we were attacked. He had been serving a sentence for rape and murder. So, I wasn't all that fond of going to the dacha anymore."

She added, "There was, however, one very good thing that happened; a wonderful and exciting experience. The first Population Control Congress run by the United Nations took place in Bucharest [Romania]. I had known about it before we left Washington for Sofia, and had asked the State Department if I could be part of the American delegation. I was told that it was already filled with high-powered experts, headed by Secretary Weinberger. So I had put it out of my mind.

"A few days before it was scheduled to begin, I got a cable signed by Henry Kissinger asking me if I would join the delegation after all.

Apparently, some women in Washington had pointed out that the delegation, which was working on population control, was made up entirely of men. Kissinger had asked around for some women to send and my name was put forward. When I arrived in Bucharest, however, I was not greeted very nicely by the other delegates. They admitted afterwards that, as the wife of an ambassador and with no other official connections, they looked on me as dead wood. But because of my previous work on population issues, I knew many of the delegates from the other countries and was able to work very effectively with them. This congress was the one good thing that happened to me in almost four years."

Chapter Seven

CIA Wives: To Love, Honor, and Take the Polygraph

They met in an Eastern European capital. She was employed by the British embassy and he was an American diplomat. After a year or so of dating, they announced their engagement. Not long before their wedding, they decided to take a trip to a neighboring Western European country, meet up with some friends, and generally take a break from the pressures of working under constant surveillance in a communist country.

She said, "On arrival at our first stop, we checked into our hotel. This is when my fiancé dropped the bombshell on me. He told me that he worked for the CIA and that we were actually on the trip for a reason other than simple fun and relaxation. In order for us to be married and for him to keep his job, I would have to be subjected to a polygraph examination as part of a security investigation of my background. I was incredulous.

"First of all, I was furious that our trip, which we had spent so much time planning, was just a ruse to get me there. Secondly, he had lied to me, not a good start to any marriage. And thirdly, I was furious that I had to be hooked up to a machine and have *my* honesty and integrity questioned. Who did these people think they were! And quite frankly, I found it insulting as a British citizen to be treated in such a disrespectful manner. Weren't we supposed to be one of America's closest friends?

"At first, I refused to take the test. However, after my fiancé pointed out to me that he would have no security clearance and therefore no job if I didn't, I reluctantly agreed. Under the security guidelines, he actually had to submit his resignation just in case I didn't pass. If that had happened, the good news was that we would be able to go ahead with our marriage, but the bad news was that neither of us would have a job because I had already handed in my resignation and he would no longer have a security clearance! Needless to say, I passed the test, but I found the whole experience quite sleazy and distasteful."

I heard variations of this story from a number of women. (The rules apply equally to male foreign-born spouses, but I am confining my discussion here to the women.) American-born spouses of CIA officers undergo background checks, but they are not polygraphed as a condition of the officers' employment. Foreign-born wives start out feeling suspect. No one I spoke with questioned the need for background investigations, but most felt that the eleventh-hour disclosure of the fiancé's true employer put them in a position of having to make a decision after all the wedding plans had been made. It felt like blackmail.

According to an Agency official, the CIA divides foreign-born spouses into two groups and treats each differently. The first group consists of those women who are foreign-born, but who were married and naturalized before their husbands applied for employment. These women are polygraphed only if the security background check indicates a problem: undesirable political affiliations or legal difficulties, for example. Because these women are already citizens, they can be fully involved in the recruitment process and are encouraged to ask their own questions. Once their husbands are hired, the women also have the opportunity to meet other employees and their wives during the training period, and to participate in orientation classes. An orientation class for spouses is held twice a year (Agency-wide) and an overseas orientation class is held several times a year for employees and spouses in the Directorate of Operations (DO) preparing for their first overseas assignments.

The second group of wives consists of those who meet their husbands after they have been employed and are already overseas on assignment. According to an Agency official: "Nothing is done to encourage these marriages." That is a nice way of saying that, driven by security regulations, the process is adversarial. It can take months for the clearances to come through, putting enormous stress on the relationship. The wives are not the only ones who are put in an unpleasant situation. Following the rules, the men are caught in the middle. As one officer observed, while his future wife's background investigation was being conducted, he felt suspect too.

Even though these are Agency rules, it is clear that many CIA wives include their husbands in the ranks of the opposition. We will never know how many marriages end before they even start because of these obstacles.

As well as having to face the polygraph before a clearance is granted, the woman also learns at this point that, unlike the wives of employees of the other foreign affairs agencies, she must become an American citizen if her husband is to be assigned overseas again. As soon as the marriage takes place, the officer's tour is curtailed, and if he wants to continue working for the Agency, the couple must return to the United States until the wife is naturalized. Many officers try to time their weddings to coincide with the end of their tours. In the 1960s, one woman's marriage led to her husband losing his job altogether.

Isabelle is from a South American country. After high school, she went to the United States for college, so she speaks English as well as Spanish. Returning to her country after graduation, she gravitated to the expatriate American community and from time to time attended parties at the Marine House. It was there that she met her future husband, an Agency communicator. "He didn't tell me where he worked and I never asked," she said. "It was not until he actually proposed about a year later that he told me. We got engaged at Christmas with the idea of getting married in January. The moment that he told the people in the office that he was engaged to me, they told him he had to hand in the keys to the commo shop and that he was not allowed to go back there. His tour was supposed to end the following summer, but when we got married in January, he had to leave the country. He told them he didn't want to quit the Agency, but they said he would have to wait until I became a citizen to be rehired. So we went back to his home state and he got a job doing something else while we waited out the three years for me to be eligible for naturalization.

"After I was naturalized, my husband was rehired and assigned immediately to go to a country in Western Europe. But there was a stipulation that I *had* to work for them! I was already a citizen and was hired on a contract as a spouse on site, so I was not polygraphed. But then they gave me the job of back-up or emergency contact for a very sensitive asset. They needed someone who spoke Spanish with no trace of an accent."

For many years there was a rule that officers could not be assigned to the native country of their spouses. This rule has been relaxed, but it still applies to some countries, if the foreign-born spouse has family still living there. For example, an applicant who would otherwise be recruited for his Chinese language and area knowledge would not be hired if he were married to a Chinese-born woman with family still living in China, because, under the guidelines, the Agency could not take advantage of his skills.

A great deal is expected of all the wives of CIA officers, American- or foreign-born. They learn very early that the need for discretion and secrecy is real. Their safety and that of their colleagues and assets depends on it. Their husbands' movements and whereabouts and the people they associate with are not topics of conversation with people who have no business knowing. That means just about everyone, including their own children.

Parents have to make their own determination about when to entrust the information of their father's employer to their children. It is up to them to make the judgment of when the child can cope with the responsibility of keeping the secret. The parents often are not helped on this issue by the non-Agency members of the embassy community, who are not discreet around their dining room tables and give their own children knowledge they should not have. Many Agency parents have been faced with a child coming home from school saying; 'So-and-so said his mother said Dad is a spy.' At that point the parents must either deny it or be forced into a conversation they would have chosen to put off until the child was older.

The need for secrecy can have a crippling effect on the wife's social relationships. Even within an embassy, her husband's Agency position is supposed to be closely held, and she has to be very good at keeping information to herself and to tolerate appearing to be uninformed or even clueless on some occasions. Unless she is extremely confident and experienced in the workings of the embassy community, she will more than likely hold herself separate. To maintain her husband's cover, she may be discouraged from befriending the wives of other officers also under cover. If she does choose her friends only from among the wives of her husband's Agency colleagues, she may be accused of cliquishness by the non-Agency wives.

If the wife is foreign-born, she can be doubly isolated, especially if she belongs to the group who joins "midstream." She has to learn the community rules, figure out who everyone is, find a place for herself, and be careful in conversation. In some cases, the husband has been known to encourage this apartness, perhaps believing that it is the easiest way to deal with the security situation. So he becomes the conduit of all information, filtering what the wife learns. If her English language skills are poor to start with, this isolation works against her in every way. On more than one occasion, I and others I spoke to have heard American-born members of the foreign-affairs community express the opinion that one of the reasons some men marry non-English-speaking women is to be in control.

One the other hand, the wife who is confident and who has the support of her husband can make contacts in the international community—often facilitated by her language skills—that are advantageous to her husband in his work. These contacts, as well as those that are purely social, must be reported and are monitored.

Christine experienced two kinds of tours. On one tour, her husband's job was so secret that he did not go near the embassy and few people knew what he was doing (including her). Fortunately, she spoke the country's language and could function on her own. On the other tour, her husband was under diplomatic cover and she was more involved: "I find it a disadvantage not to know. At the first post, I didn't know where he was going and he was gone a lot. The children always asked, 'Oh, is Dad coming late tonight again?' I would tell them that he'd be gone a certain number of days, always kind of up in the air. It was not easy, but they got used to it and they don't question it any more. At the other post, my husband and I could go for a walk and talk about more things. I liked that. I knew what I had to look out for and I found that interesting. Sometimes I would give my opinion about something or someone and it would turn out that I was right."

At least in a diplomatic community, there is contact with the husband's workplace. In Washington, D.C., there is very little, and a tour there can be isolating. There is virtually no way that an Agency wife can be informed about regulations, classes, or other spouse events, except through her husband. She has to have a great deal of trust that the assignment options he brings home are the only ones open, and that conditions at post are as presented.

Often the only time Agency family members have the opportunity to visit the CIA's Family Liaison Office is right before an overseas assignment, during medical clearance checkups. This office works closely with the State facilities—the Family Liaison Office and the Overseas Briefing Center—and publicizes courses held there to its employees. But again, this information has to be carried home by the employee. Many Agency wives seem reluctant to use the State Department resources because they worry about questions that might be asked of them. Or they have been convinced that the Agency and the Department are unconnected and hostile. Some do not realize that almost everything that affects State Department wives affects them too, and it is to their advantage to keep abreast of regulations, to learn coping skills, to research their own employment options, and to join and support the Associates of the American Foreign Service Worldwide (AAFSW), whose activities benefit family members of all agencies.

In a few cases related to me, it seemed that Agency regulations concerning foreign-born wives were not clearly understood by some employees, or that the Agency used the wife's foreign-born status as an excuse for a decision. For example, one foreign-born wife, who had been married for some years before her husband joined the Agency and had been naturalized before they left Washington on their first overseas assignment, was denied employment as a typist in the station by Headquarters because she "had not been a citizen long enough." The chief of station argued the absurdity of the ruling and she eventually was hired.

Another foreign-born wife had worked as a contract employee for the Agency on and off for thirteen years. During one of her husband's Washington assignments, she applied to be a staff employee. Permanent staff status was to her advantage because she would be eligible for the employee spouse program, which stipulates that if no job is available for her overseas in the station to which her husband has been assigned, her Washington job must be held for her for five years. Otherwise, she would have to start from scratch as a new job applicant and lose any accrued benefits. Initially, the wife was refused because "she had family still living in a foreign country." That foreign country was the United Kingdom. Her foreign-born status was used, erroneously, in an attempt to deny her this advantage. It was sorted out eventually, but her resentment level had risen just another notch.

In another incident, a wife received expeditious naturalization in preparation for her husband's overseas assignment. When the assignment fell through, a staff member suggested that her citizenship be revoked.

The foreign-born wives I spoke to have, over the years, reconciled themselves to life with the CIA: the long working hours and their husbands' frequent absences. Some have subsequently chosen to work for the Agency themselves, with a kind of "if you can't beat 'em, join 'em" attitude. CIA officers, in general, are extremely driven, and engaged in what they will often refer to as "God's work" of protecting the interests of the United States. It is difficult for a wife to argue with a divine calling without seeming less than committed herself. Most of the women felt that more could be done to support them in a life that is often stressful. They said that introducing them to their husbands' Agency affiliation with less unpleasantness would have helped them to start their association with the Agency on a more positive note.

Bibi's Story

A Diplomatic Life

Life in the American foreign service brought few surprises to Bibi because she had grown up in the diplomatic world. Her father, a close friend of Nehru's, served as India's ambassador to Burma, Japan, Canada, Luxembourg, Belgium, and Switzerland. "My family came originally from Uttar Pradesh," Bibi said. "I was born in 1943 and am the sixth of ten children. I always felt very sorry for the Indian government because going on transfers was like moving a small village: children, servants, dogs, and cats. My parents moved from country to country without having a posting back in India, so I never went to school there. I attended whatever school was available where we were posted, and where there was none, I was tutored at home.

"Even though I was brought up abroad and allowed to date non-Indians, it was always made clear to me that I was going to be married to an Indian of my parents' choice. When I was nineteen, my marriage was arranged to a first cousin, a common practice in Muslim families such as ours.

"At the time of my marriage, my father was ambassador to Switzerland. My husband was a student in Cambridge, Massachusetts, and immediately after our wedding in Bern, I went to live with him in Cambridge. I taught at a small school for a year or two and left when my daughter was born. Later, our son was born there as well.

"My husband's field is rocket science and after he finished his studies, he worked for an American firm. Then NASA [National Aeronautics and Space Administration] encouraged him to become an American citizen so that he could get a clearance to work on classified projects for them. So we became citizens in 1975 and he went to work for NASA.

"During a visit to Washington, a friend of ours mentioned that the State Department was looking for a science counselor to go to India. We thought that would be fun, so my husband applied for the position. He was hired on loan to the State Department and sent to the embassy in New Delhi in 1983 as the counselor for science and technology. Our children were already away at college so did not accompany us.

"When we returned to Washington from Delhi, my husband actually joined the foreign service and we have since been posted to Mexico and South Korea."

Chapter Eight

A Place to Go—Marital Problems and Divorce

Not long after my husband and I were married and were living in the United States near his parents, my mother-in-law said to me, "If ever you feel you need to leave, you can come here. Everybody needs a place to go." Considering the fact that the person I would be leaving was her son, I thought it was a pretty generous offer. She knew that going home to my own mother would have been an expensive and extremely disruptive option, especially as a temporary measure. My husband used to joke that he had to make sure I was happy because he could not afford to have me do that. I never had to take my mother-in-law up on her offer, but it was nice to know that she recognized my need to have options.

With their own families far away, foreign service couples living abroad have to look elsewhere for support. In an embassy community, there is definitely the feeling of living in a fishbowl. Many women are reluctant to discuss their personal problems with other women in the embassy because they are the wives of their husbands' colleagues. Wives of senior officers have even fewer options for friendship. The embassy doctor and nurse practitioner are available for consultation, but they are usually also social acquaintances. Even though they are professional people and trained to be discreet, there is always the issue of the personal relationship and the feeling that nothing in the embassy is ever really private.

A visit from a State Department psychiatrist who makes periodic rounds of the embassies in a particular region can be unsatisfactory as well. Notification of a visit is relayed through the employees, and wives may not hear about it, or even if they do, they may feel constrained from signing up. Certainly, it would be hard to do so without their husbands' knowledge.

While on a Washington, D.C., assignment, employees and family members can contact the Employee Consultation Service in the State Department, which provides short-term counseling and referrals. It is a free service staffed by licensed clinical social workers. But the issue of privacy comes up again. Many women are just unwilling to talk about their problems with their husbands' employer.

If the problems lead to separation or divorce, wives also can call the Family Liaison Office (FLO), which employs a support services officer who acts as a referral source of information. Women I spoke to were more willing to contact this office to find out what options they had. Alternatively, while on a Washington assignment, wives can obtain a measure of privacy by consulting doctors and counselors not connected with the State Department.

The foreign-born foreign service wife is away from her family supports both in Washington and at post. In many cultures, discussing one's personal problems with anyone but a family member is unthinkable, so problems are suppressed and not resolved, adding to a foreign wife's feeling of isolation.

Michele remembers coping with the stresses of separation from family, of motherhood, of a frequently absent husband, and of a new culture. She had sensed problems while overseas, but she was reluctant to talk about them, and it was not until her husband was assigned to Washington that she was forced to confront them.

She remembered, "I had viral pneumonia, the kids had walking pneumonia, and my husband said, 'I have to go overseas.' He left on the trip and I was incapacitated for about two months; brushing my teeth was a struggle. I was in bad, bad shape. A friend came to help me and brought me food. She said, 'Michele, you have to do something about this. You are depressed! You have got to see a psychiatrist.' She was my neighbor and a wonderful woman, but I thought, 'How dare you!' I thought that seeing a psychiatrist was the equivalent of going naked in the street. Besides, this was 1970 and I couldn't tell my friends that I went to see a psychiatrist. Or the State Department. What would that do to my husband's career! She said, 'You've got to help yourself.'

"So I did, and it was the best thing I did in my life. It enabled me to put things in perspective. All the things I had to deal with, marriage, leaving home, motherhood. The depression had gotten bigger and bigger and was not acknowledged. Also, the dependency I had built up on my mother. I am an only child. Since leaving my parents I had written a letter every day, not necessarily a long one, but on a daily basis, and my mother practically did the same thing. And, of course, with the children growing older, it was becoming quite a burden. The psychiatrist helped me put a perspective on this dependency I had on my mother, that I was hanging on to being a child. All these things combined led to depression.

"It was very, very scary. I think that the taboo is not there any more. Americans are more open-minded about psychiatry. The French still are not. When I told my parents, my mother felt that I was crazy. To dare to go to a psychiatrist, I had to be crazy. She couldn't understand why I was doing it. I told her, 'I go to the dentist when my tooth aches. I am going to a psychiatrist because my soul aches and I've got to do something about it.'

"I could never have discussed this with anyone else. I was French and you don't wash your dirty linen in public, so that was part of my handicap. Talking about your husband is like a betrayal, and you just didn't do that. Eventually, I felt free to talk about it with the psychiatrist.

"This is the time that I was able to remove the safety pins from the curtains. To be able to breathe freely and not have this immense feeling of inadequacy of not being able to cope with everything that came up."

Bibi's marital problems sprang from the differing attitudes toward women that she and her husband had developed from their families. Although they came from the same Muslim Indian family, the women on her side were encouraged to speak up, while those on her husband's side were not. American culture reinforced Bibi's point of view. She also found the life of an American housewife to be a difficult one. She said, "The American woman has to be on par with her husband intellectually and socially. She has to keep a very nice house, cook and clean. We couldn't afford household help. I remember I wrote back to my mother the first year I got married, 'I didn't realize I had so many muscles in my body because I can now feel them.' I had never worked so hard in my life. And you had to maintain a certain standard and all within a budget. The children had to have help with their homework. It was very difficult. By the time you finished all those tasks, you didn't have time to sit and talk to your husband.

"Our marriage improved when we were assigned to India and could afford to employ servants. They removed work from me so that I could spend some quality time with my husband. I think one of the reasons marriages here have much more strain is because of that. The very reason you get married, to be together, is what the marriage takes away. You are never together."

When the subject of divorce came up in my conversations, almost everyone had stories about women they had known over the years, some of whom had been left destitute after long marriages. Many of these situations occurred before the AAFSW was able to secure pension rights for divorced foreign service spouses in the 1980s.[1]

However, even though women now are guaranteed a percentage of their ex-husbands' pensions when they retire, subject to certain conditions, many are still disadvantaged financially because they have not been able to sustain paid employment as they moved around the world. In addition, the atmosphere in which foreign service wives previously were judged in a divorce settlement has not changed. An attitude prevails that they have had an easy life to which they contribute nothing of financial value. One woman reported that the judge actually stated this when ruling in her property settlement hearing in Fairfax County in the 1990s.

Because of the nature of foreign service life, divorce can be complicated, especially when children are involved. It is particularly complicated for the foreign-born spouse. One woman I interviewed was overseas at post when her husband announced that (after fifteen years of marriage) he wanted a divorce and had requested a curtailment of his assignment so that they could all return to Washington. The Deputy Chief of Mission

(DCM), who, within the embassy is the person charged with the responsibility to make such decisions,[2] granted the curtailment and ordered the family back to Washington.

The woman, who retained her original citizenship, had spent little time in the United States. Faced with divorce, she wanted to return to the family home in her own country with her two children. When she initiated legal proceedings in the city where they were posted, the embassy claimed diplomatic immunity for the husband. This meant that the local authorities could do nothing for her. A letter from the embassy informed the woman that she was free to do what she wanted, but the children would be returning to the United States with their father. Within days, the family was on a plane back to Washington.

Without family in the Washington area, the woman stayed alone in a hotel for the first few days. Through a church and The Women's Center in Vienna, Virginia, she obtained legal advice. Eventually, she won joint legal custody and full physical custody of the children. However, by court order, her husband holds the children's passports, which she must request in writing when she wants to travel outside the United States with the children.

After the family left the post, embassy employees packed up the household effects and shipped them to the husband. The woman had no direct access to her own belongings. (When a family's household effects are shipped or stored by the U.S. government, the employee's name is on the paperwork. In order to gain access to either, the spouse must have a signed power of attorney from the employee or a valid court order.[3] Similarly, if a spouse wants to leave post in the event of marital problems, any belongings she wants to take with her will not be shipped by the government unless the employee signs the papers.)

Fortunately, this woman's English is fluent and, through a job skills program organized by the county in which she lives, she was able to find employment. With what she earns and the court-ordered child support she receives from her husband, she can afford to rent a two-bedroom apartment for herself and her children. She does not own a car.

It was obvious from my conversations about divorce that money was again a central problem for the women. It went from being an issue of cultural approach to one of survival. The stories I heard were of women who had no direct access to the family's accounts and knew nothing about their investments. Women were given allowances, or ATM cards for household expenses, or checks made out to stores for groceries. At one post, alarmed by their ignorance of financial matters, the CLO was moved to hold a workshop to explain the basics of family finances and credit issues to the foreign-born wives.

Without family nearby, foreign-born foreign service wives must be resourceful when it comes to protecting themselves in the event of marital problems. It is imperative that they learn the rules and regulations of the foreign service, especially those concerning health-care coverage and pension and property rights. They should have money put aside for emergencies. They should also be aware that if their marriages fail, they will not legally be able to return to their native countries with their children without the agreement of their husbands. It is also important that they maintain personal connections in the Washington area so that in an emergency they have a place to go.

Chapter Nine

Family Ties

As I was conducting my interviews, I looked for patterns or themes that were common among the women. I wondered if there were some quality they shared which gave them the courage to take the step of leaving their countries and following their husbands to the United States. At the time of their marriages, few of the women seemed to feel that they were taking a risk that was any greater than that involved in any marriage. They were in love, they wanted to be with their husbands, and if that meant leaving their countries, they would do so. In retrospect, several thought that a pre-wedding trip to the United States to meet his family and friends would have been a good idea and they would recommend such a trip to others. But at the time, reservations voiced by their own relatives, such as 'How do you know he's not already married?' were brushed aside.

In her book *Intercultural Marriage*, Dugan Romano suggests that there are certain types of people who are more likely to look for marriage partners outside their own cultures: romantics, who find their own kind uninteresting and look for adventure; compensators, who look to fill a void in their own personalities; rebels, who protest their own societies; internationals, who have already lived outside their own countries for various reasons; and non-traditionals and others, who do not fit into their own societies for any number of reasons.[1] Examples of several of these groups emerged among the women I interviewed: daughters of diplomats who moved from country to country and stayed for only short periods in their own countries (although Bibi married a fellow Indian); daughters of cross-cultural marriages in societies where this was a disadvantage; women who by the standards of their cultures were beyond desirable marriageable age; and women who had already made the break from their own cultures by living and working in other countries. Differences from their peers may have been a factor in their obtaining permission from parents who otherwise might have objected to a foreign marriage, but the women did not seem to have been actively looking for a spouse from another culture.

Their backgrounds were remarkable for their differences, rather than for their similarities. The women had different levels of education and had lived with their husbands in different countries and at different times. The one connection the women shared seemed to be just the fact that they were married to American foreign service officers.

As I listened for common threads, however, I began to hear repeated references to their mothers. With only a few exceptions, the women had been very close to their mothers at the time of their marriages and, one way or another, maintained close contact after they left home. Rather than binding them, the close ties freed them to make the choices they made. Even the women who were only children were able to leave because of the positive attitude and continuing support of their mothers.

Inger was the only daughter. She said, "I was the youngest of three: my two brothers were eleven and fifteen years older than me. My mother was forty when I was born. She was a wonderful mother, typical of her generation, at home and caring. Her father was a minister of education in Denmark, but she and her four sisters were never allowed an education because the attitude was that they would marry and have children. My father died three months before I got married. My mother never once said, 'You can't' or 'You shouldn't leave.' She said she would rather see me happily married outside of Denmark than unhappily married in Denmark. It was very generous of her, I don't know if I would be able to be so generous with my own daughter."

Maggy's father died when she was small. Her mother was twenty-nine when he died and was left with four children. As the law in Belgium stipulated at the time, Maggy and her siblings were assigned a male tutor to oversee their upbringing. "My brother and I were sent to boarding school," she said. "After four years, I came home to stay and, as the eldest, was my mother's confidante. She always told us that as long as it was honest, the four of us could do whatever we wanted to do with our lives, and she stuck to it. She cried when my husband and I left after our wedding but we promised to come back. In those days, it was expensive to travel and the allowances were different, but we tried to travel through Europe on our way to and from our postings. She also traveled to see us right up until just before she died at seventy-nine."

Elisabeth was at loggerheads with her father most of her life but she was very close to her mother. She said, "When I went home to Vienna after meeting Martin at Alpbach, I only told my mother and my best friend about my engagement. Through all the struggles to earn money to put myself through school in opposition to my father's wishes, my mother never stopped believing in me. We were very close."

I have also enjoyed the continuing encouragement and support of my mother. When I first left Sydney in 1966 and was in London and Europe, we wrote letters because phone calls were very expensive. (She has kept all the letters I have written to her since 1966.) On my first day at the World Bank in Washington, D.C., I received a bouquet of flowers from a local florist, which my mother had sent to welcome me to my new job. When my first daughter was born in 1971, my mother made her first visit to the United States. Since then, she has traveled alone or with my stepfather to almost every place we have lived, in the United States and overseas. She also came for my younger daughter's birth, both christenings, graduations, and my older daughter's wedding. Through letters, birthday cards, and gifts, she has maintained a relationship with her granddaughters in spite of the distance between them. Today, they communicate via e-mail. She has met our friends, several of whom have called on her when they have been in Sydney. When I was naturalized, I worried that my family would be unhappy about it, but to my relief, my mother said, 'Your life is there now; your husband and children are Americans, so it makes sense for you to be an American too.' Having this support, even at a distance, has been extremely important to me, as it has been to the other women.

Many of the women have made a point of visiting their families as funds and time allowed, sending their children to them for vacations and inviting them to visit wherever they were posted. In many cases, home-sickness has meant missing family, not country.

As the years go by, and the mothers (and fathers) age, their care becomes a concern. This is actually an important issue for all members of the foreign service who serve in countries far from their parents' homes. It is possible to take elderly relatives overseas as dependents. They can be included in the employee's orders, issued diplomatic passports, and granted the same diplomatic immunity as a spouse or a child. If the relatives are not financially dependent, they can still go as tourists but receive no official government support.[2]

In 1998, the AAFSW convened an interagency conference to discuss eldercare for all members of the foreign service. It was generally agreed that taking aging relatives to post was not the best solution, especially where medical facilities were not adequate for their care. The agency representatives discussed how travel regulations could be modified to help families care for aging parents who remained at home. Extra trips are now authorized for employees and their eligible spouses who are serving overseas.[3]

Rekha's mother lives in Madras, India, and her brother lives nearby. She said, "Our overseas posts were all in countries around India and we had my mother come visit us, both to give her a different experience and because it made more sense and was cheaper than the four of us traveling to see her. Several years ago, I asked her if she would like to come and live with us, and she said no, that everyone would just go away in the morning and she would be alone all day. Her life is there. In recent years I have traveled to see her once a year. It's difficult being so far away because you feel helpless. You also feel you are not doing your fair share to support your sibling, who may or may not be doing things as you would do them. You lose your right to criticize because you are not a full participant."

Tanja (who is an only child) and her husband also have invited her mother to live with them, but her mother declined for the same reasons. She does not speak English, so it would be an isolating experience for her.

"She loves to visit us and be near our children, but in Zagreb she has her own friends and social life," Tanja said.

Bo-Yeon travels to Seoul once or twice a year to visit her family. She spends most of the time with her father, who is eighty-one and in poor health. Long-since reconciled to her decision to leave home and be independent, he now calls her his pioneer. She said, "My sisters and brothers who live in Seoul cannot talk back to him, but he takes it from me. When they can't get him to take medicine or drink more water, I will tell him that he should because it's good for him, and he will do what I say. When I go back to visit, I have to stay near him for the first week and then little by little, I can leave to go out to have lunch with friends or stay a night or two with my sisters.

"My mother, who is ten years younger than my father, suffers from diabetes. One year, when she was not following her diet strictly enough, the family sent her to live with me for a few months. I watched over what she ate, and her health improved, but as soon as she went home, she started eating candy again."

Bo-Yeon added, "My children sometimes ask me why I don't go to Seoul more often to be with my parents now that they are old. Besides the fact that it's expensive to travel there, I try to explain that my first responsibility is to them and their father. Who is going to drive my son to all his after-school activities if I am not here? It is difficult to balance between your parents and your own family when you live so far away."

Another foreign-born spouse made increasingly frequent visits to see her aging parents. She joked that, although her visits gave some respite to her brother who lived nearby, her parents probably breathed a sigh of relief when she left. She would swoop in, try to bring her idea of order to their house and their eating schedules, and then leave.

Some of the women found that their cultural attitudes toward the care of aging parents were at odds with American culture. Their husbands and their parents-in-law were more used to the idea of independence from their children and preferred nursing home care when they could no longer live by themselves. They did not want to be a burden to their children.

Wati comes from a large family and her parents are no longer living. Her concern is for her own old age: "Old age for people in the United States seems to be very lonely. They are not surrounded by grandchildren and nephews and nieces; they are on their own. When I see older people walking alone, I miss my home. If they were in Indonesia, there would be someone walking with them, a neighbor or a servant, son or daughter, somebody to look after them. We don't let the elderly walk on their own. It's a matter of respect that the younger ones should accompany the old. So I often wonder if I would like to stay here or go back to Indonesia. It's not very easy for me to accept the idea of a nursing home."

Didem's mother is still young, but Didem worries about the future. "I just don't have the answer," she said. "My mother speaks no English and her life and friends are there in Istanbul. It would be very difficult for her here. But in my culture, when you are older you go to live with your family. It's unheard of, to go to a nursing home. I was discussing this with my mother-in-law and she told me that when the time comes we should put her in a nursing home. When I said that I thought she should live with us, she was kind of speechless. Even my husband looked at me. Yes, she would be alone during the day because I work too, but we would be together at night and in the mornings. Somebody would be there to take care of her. I think having an older person in the house would also be good for my daughter."

Hala's parents fled the war in Lebanon in 1976 and came to live in the United States. She said, "It was wonderful having them here when we came back between assignments overseas, especially because my daughter was able to have a relationship with them. Foreign service children often don't have the chance to develop close relationships with their grandparents. But when my father got sick, it was harder that we were in the States in one way because there was just my mother and me to take care of him. In Lebanon, we would have had the whole family to help."

It is clear from my conversations with the women that most of them were not leaving their countries to escape family. Some had already chosen to travel and live outside their own countries because they were curious, but most probably would have stayed or returned home if they had not married as they did. Their relationships with their families remained important to them, especially the relationships with their mothers.

No matter how close the emotional relationship is, living far away from aging parents decreases the amount of participation the women can have in their care. Many of the women said they dread the phone call in the night, followed by a dash to the airport. They fear that the call will come too late and that they will not arrive in time to say good-bye. For most foreign-born spouses, this situation exists whether the family is overseas or in the United States.

Virginia's Story

A Continuing Journey

The voice on the telephone was soft but confident, the English fluent, and the accent slight and hard to place. She was calling in response to a notice I had put in the AAFSW newsletter seeking contributions from wives born in Africa. Her name was Virginia, she came from Gabon, and she offered to tell me her story. We met (in the summer of 2000) at the apartment where she was living temporarily with her husband and son in northern Virginia. Her husband, who is from Minnesota, had just completed his A-100 class, had taken a refresher course in the French language, and was preparing for his first assignment, as an administrative officer, to Abidjan, Ivory Coast.

Virginia and her husband met in 1988 in her village in Gabon, where he had been sent by the Peace Corps to help families raise fish. Her mother was the head of the family of six: Virginia and her four brothers and one sister. He was in his early twenties and she was eighteen, already the mother of a four-year-old son. Her native language is Fang, but she had learned French in school. This was their only common language because she spoke no English.

Through a close working relationship, he became part of her family. But when Virginia wanted to leave with him when the Peace Corps transferred him to another rural area in Gabon and then to the capital (which she had never even visited before), it was hard for her family to accept. Liking him was one thing, but allowing Virginia to leave and make her life with him was quite another. In the end, her mother gave permission.

When his assignment to Gabon was over, he took Virginia to the United States to introduce her to his family and to his country. She had already met his mother and sisters when they had visited Gabon. At that time, she still spoke no English and he had had to translate for everyone. After that, his mother took French lessons so that she could communicate with Virginia herself. In the United States, he bought a van, and for six months they traveled around the country visiting other Peace Corps volunteers they had known in Africa.

They were married in Minnesota in 1994. She is Catholic and he is Lutheran and neither of them wanted to change, so they had a small wedding at home blessed by a priest. Her son stayed in Gabon with her brother for three years while the couple was getting settled. Her husband worked several different jobs and was then rehired by the Peace Corps as a staff employee in Minneapolis.

At first, when Virginia went out by herself, her husband would write a note for her to give to the bus driver explaining where she wanted to get off. She started watching television and taking English as a Second Language classes. She worked her way to a level where she could enroll in classes to earn a high school diploma. Taking five and six classes at a time, she received her diploma in 1999. "One of my dreams was to get an education, and moving here gave me that opportunity," she said. "In that sense, America is a dream country. From television shows, people think that everybody in the United States is rich, but they don't realize that people here work hard for what they have. I didn't expect anybody to give me anything; I knew I had to work for what I wanted."

While studying, she was also working full time. With no job experience, she started as a housekeeper in a hotel. She soon realized that that was not work she wanted to do for very long, so when her English improved, she applied for a job as a salesperson at one of the large department stores in Minneapolis. With constant customer contact, her English improved even more.

When she and her husband both had steady work and had bought a house, Virginia went back to Gabon and picked up her son. He is fifteen now and speaks English. He has started also taking French in school and is doing well and making friends.

After her husband was accepted by the foreign service, they sold their house in Minneapolis and moved to the Washington area for training. "It was hard to leave Minnesota," she said. "I consider it to be my home in the U.S., and I would like the chance to go back there, even if it is the coldest place in the country. We had our first house there and I had a flower and vegetable garden in the summer. I was very happy and I learned so much there.

"I have not attended any foreign service training with my husband. I am taking college classes and don't have time. But I did go to the Overseas Briefing Center a couple of times and pick up a lot of information. My husband tells me what he learns, especially about the security issues and about what things will be like in the embassy. It's not like the Peace Corps. We'll have a house rented by the government and live with other Americans.

"While we are living in Abidjan, I would like to bring my mother from Gabon to stay with us for a long vacation. She works very hard. We talk on the telephone from time to time but she can't read, so my letters have to be read to her by someone else."

Virginia became an American citizen in 1999 in Minnesota, an event she described as overwhelming: "One of the reasons I wanted to become a citizen was so that I could vote. This year will be my first time and I can't wait. At the end of the year, we will leave for Africa. I am very excited about going back and representing the United States there."

Chapter Ten

Life after the Foreign Service

Although Washington, D.C., may be just another post in the early years, many couples do eventually retire there, especially if the husband continues to work in the field of foreign affairs after retirement from the foreign service. Because Washington is one of the most culturally diverse areas in the United States, many of the foreign-born wives prefer to stay there if the alternative is to retire in small towns in other parts of the country in which their husbands grew up and to which some of them would like to return.

Inger experienced reentry along with the retirement of her husband when they returned to Washington to stay. Reentry is a term used in the foreign service to describe coming home. For some people, the experience actually does resemble the act of reentering the earth's atmosphere from outer space that the term conjures up.

She said, "We had been gone for sixteen years all together with only short vacations here in between, so when we came back, I found everything had changed and the people we used to know had, of course, gone their own way. I knew nobody. I felt absolutely as if I had been put under a cheese bell and my life had come to a screeching, scary halt. My husband's colleagues were all retired, so here I was, forty years old, dealing with their wives who were sixty-five, and I did not have a whole lot in common with them. Plus, I had been stripped of all the networks I had overseas and the special place I occupied in the communities we lived in. And who am I to tell about it? My Danish friends would say, 'Can't hack it, huh? You are spoiled by all that fancy living.' But it wasn't exactly that; I had no one to talk to about the things that mattered to me. Overseas, I had access; in Washington, people are not going to talk to you unless you can do something for them.

"I must have told my husband once a week that I wanted to go back to Denmark, but he convinced me that it was better for us to stay here. It took me two years to pick myself up. The thing that helped me was working with SOS International, the medical emergency evacuation service. I made lots of trips for them to Scandinavia and in the process had the chance to see what life was like in Denmark for my friends and relatives. Eventually, I realized that the United States is where I belong. It took me a long time, but having adjusted to so many other countries, I adjusted again.

"My experience coming back here has sharpened my survival skills, and I use them in my work. Because the health field is such a business in the United States, it is a tough place to work. Danish doctors and nurses will accept situations that I will not. For example, when faced with getting a patient out of a hospital or clinic and to the airport on schedule, I will say, 'If you think that patient is dehydrated and cannot travel for two days it's your bloody fault, because you've had him in intensive care for three weeks. You get him up to snuff, because we're leaving at eight o'clock tonight.' However, the moment I get to the boarding gate with SAS, I have to reverse. If I use my American tools in a Scandinavian setting, it works against me. So I have learned how best to function in both places."

She continued, "We've been back ten years now. We bought a house in Virginia, which I absolutely love and if I'm not working or traveling, I'm right here with my husband and my dog. This is my refuge and I will never move again. Never. Not even to Denmark at this point. For a visit, yes, any time, but not to live. I am settled and content here."

Maria Bauer and her husband now live in Washington, but when he first retired from the U.S. Information Service (USIS) some years ago, he took a teaching position at Kenyon College in Ohio. Maria said, "I was in favor of his taking the job although it meant moving again. But I went into a deep depression because it was the first time the children were both gone—my daughter was married and my son was away at school. I went to see a doctor, not a psychiatrist, to get some sleeping pills because I couldn't sleep, and discussed my depression with him. My husband and I were living in a house rented from another professor away on sabbatical; I had never lived in a small town before, only in capitals; I didn't know anybody; and I didn't want to get involved with ladies' social life any more. The doctor said, 'Think of something you have wanted to do all your life and never had time to do and do it.' That was when I started to write my book."[1]

Michele and her husband also have retired in the Washington area. Her concern was employment. Like Maria, she had been a full-time wife and mother and by the time of her husband's retirement her children had left home. "I have been married for thirty-six years, thirty of them in the foreign service," she said. "After we came back to Washington to stay, I had no résumé and no Social Security. When you are overseas, you have a role to play and you can play it well or less well, but you get no recognition and certainly no pay. A State Department inspector once told me that the honor of representing the country abroad should be enough for wives. But as the French say, 'That doesn't put butter on the spinach.' When we came back, I found a job as a telephone operator at a private school in Washington and am now the registrar at another. I think Social Security should be paid for wives overseas even if it comes out of their husbands' paychecks. If that were done, I would have thirty years' worth instead of only eight."

Hala and her husband are back in Washington to stay. She said, "When we were overseas in the Arab world, I didn't feel the need when I got back to Washington to have a lot of Arab friends. I wanted to be with my American friends. But now I feel the need to have a mixture. I can be totally American and I can be totally Arab. In a way, I have the best of both worlds, but there is something about me that my American friends, whom I get along with very well and whom I love dearly, can never fully know about me because they are not of a mixed culture. When I am with my Arab-American friends, there is a commonality we don't have to speak of."

Some of the women who were divorced or widowed also chose to stay in Washington, either because they owned a home there, because they found work they enjoyed, or because it was the only place in the country they knew.

Anna Maria and her husband returned to Washington from Sao Paulo, Brazil, in 1995. A year later he was diagnosed with lung cancer and died in 1997. Anna Maria chose to remain in the house they had bought years before in northwest Washington.

"I am very comfortable in Washington. My neighbors are extremely friendly and I love the area where I live. During my husband's illness and after his death, I received a lot of support from the friends we made overseas. Some of them still pass through Washington from time to time, so we keep in touch. If I were to go back to Italy, I don't think I would have that opportunity. I haven't lived in Rome for over twenty years, I don't own any property there, and I am not close to my brothers. As a widow, I am more comfortable here, where there are so many single women. I can go out alone and not feel out of place. I continue to invite people to my home as I always used to do and I continue to be invited back. Definitely, I have lost many of my husband's work friends, but there was no reason for those associations to continue in most cases anyway. I also appreciate everything that works in the States. Like when you want to complain about something, you pick up the phone and actually somebody, machine or not, gets back to you."

When Elisabeth and Martin Herz returned to Washington in 1977 after his ambassadorship to Bulgaria ended, they found themselves in limbo. He was sixty and supposed to retire, but a class action was in progress to change the retirement age rule and he wanted to stay and work towards it. Eventually, however, he took the position of diplomat in residence at Georgetown University and, with Ellsworth Bunker, helped establish the Institute for the Study of Diplomacy in the School of Foreign Service. Elisabeth was fifty-two and suffering from a depression that had started in Sofia.

"I had been away from medicine for four years, my mother had just died, and my husband's position was uncertain," she said. "I had to do something. After thinking over my options, I decided to do what I had been planning to do before I left Vienna: to get training in psychiatry so that I could combine it with the ob/gyn field and treat mind and body together.

"When I looked into it in Washington, I found that there was no psychosomatic training, and the only way I could do it was the hard way, like a newly graduated physician, and do a complete three-year residency in psychiatry. Once again, I was lucky. The Department of Psychiatry at George Washington University Hospital only took four residents each year, and one of them had just dropped out. GW has a very busy emergency room, and three residents were not enough to cover all the night work. They needed somebody immediately, and after an interview with the professor of residents' training, I was accepted. The chairman of the department never spoke to me, however. He looked on me as a fill-in until they could find someone else. At one of the social occasions, he referred to me as a nurse, although he knew full well what I was doing.

"And, doing at fifty-two what one would normally do at twenty-five was exhausting. There were times in the early hours of the morning, after dealing with psychotic and suicidal patients, when I felt that I couldn't go on. But then I would consider my alternatives and give myself a kick and go home and come back the next day. Although I was older than the other residents, I had life experience and a very profound medical background. Plus, after so many years away, I was eager and like a sponge absorbing everything. I eventually became chief resident and everything worked out.

"In the last year of my residency, the chairman of the ob/gyn department was able to convince the chairman of psychiatry to allow me to open a program for psychosomatic illnesses in the ob/gyn department. He put an interdisciplinary team together: a geneticist; an infertility specialist; a high-risk pregnancy specialist, and me. It was a marvelous team and a wonderful environment in which to work.

"But, at about the same time that I was finishing my residency, in 1980, my husband was diagnosed with cancer. He underwent surgery but suffered a recurrence a year later. He had other surgeries but they were just palliative to prolong his life. In 1983, during the last three months of his life, I wanted to stay at home, but he insisted that I continue working. I was just building up my program and he knew that the only thing that would help me over his death would be medicine. We had someone coming in to take care of him during the day, and at night I nursed him myself. We were fighting for every day. Finally he died, and two days later I was at work again.

"Over the last year of his illness, our social life had disappeared and many of our diplomatic friends had moved away. My closest friend, Carol Laise, whose husband, Ellsworth Bunker, died a year after Martin, lived within walking distance of my apartment in Washington and we saw each other as often as our work allowed. She herself was diagnosed with cancer, and died in 1991.[2] The same year, I asked for a year's sabbatical from the department at GW and went back to Vienna."

Chapter Eleven

Going Back

When I first returned to Sydney in 1969 to prepare for my wedding, I had been away two and a half years. Friends and family greeted me at the airport and we all went home for breakfast. (Flights from the United States arrived very early in the morning.) As I picked up my knife and fork to eat, I realized that everyone was watching me. Apparently, before my arrival, they had joked among themselves about whether I would now eat with my fork in my right hand as Americans typically do. We laughed together about it.

On subsequent visits I felt under similar scrutiny, especially with respect to my accent. My speaking voice, which to Americans sounded so foreign, was to Australians noticeably American. It was not a compliment to "sound like a Yank" and I felt very self-conscious when speaking to certain uncles and cousins. Not that they had anything against Americans, but for me to sound like anyone other than an Australian was taken as a sign of affectation, something that Australians take a dim view of in anybody. It was important to them that I remain "the same old Marg."

But nothing stays exactly the same, and inevitably I am no longer "the girl who used to be me." Unlike Shirley Valentine, I do not lament the changes, but there is a certain feeling of guilt attached to this process that is unshakeable. Others have experienced the same feelings.

When Carmen married in 1997 and left Chile to live in Washington, her mother made her promise to go back to visit after one year. During that year Carmen went through the normal periods of homesickness and longing for familiar foods, but she was happy. She talked often with her family by telephone and so kept up-to-date with their activities. At the end of the year, she and her husband made plans to visit Santiago. She recalled, "I looked forward to going to a particular restaurant: I told myself, 'I'm going to eat this, I'm going to eat that. I'm going to buy some clothes in my favorite stores in Santiago' because I couldn't find anything I liked in Washington. Well—the restaurant was closed the day I went, and the clothes in the department stores did not look as good as I had remembered them.

"My husband stayed two weeks and then I stayed an extra week with my mother. I made contact with some of my friends. Some I saw, some I spoke with on the phone. By the third week we had caught up with everything. They were really happy to see me, but they were also busy doing their stuff, and I had nothing to do. It became boring, I missed my husband, and I couldn't wait to get back to Washington.

"I have Chilean friends who are always going back to visit their families. I sometimes feel guilty because I don't feel the need to do that any more. I have become more independent and I'm busy with my life here."

Latha described her experiences going home: "I panicked when I went back to visit India for the first time after two years in the U.S. Going back, I wondered, 'Would I be able to converse with my mother in Marathi?' I speak and think in English even though I am not a native-speaker of the language. Growing up, I spoke English with my father and siblings and with most of my relatives. However, I spoke Marathi with my mother. While in India I could switch quite easily from one language to the other, but in the U.S. I found myself unable to speak my mother tongue, because I did not have the cultural cues. When I called to talk to my mother on the telephone, I could not utter a single world in that language. In order to fit in in the United States, I had also made a conscious effort to drop all the Indian phrases that are so much a part of 'Indian English.'

"When I first saw my mother at the airport, I kept speaking in English, but by the time we arrived at the house, I was speaking my mother tongue, as well as greeting the servants in Tamil, and my English had reverted to the Indian version. It was as if I had shed my American cloak. I was afraid of offending my family with the westernized version of myself.

"Indians love arguments; they love to discuss politics. When in India, I try to stay away from political discussions, especially about the United

States. I remember being baited by a family member and I found myself defending the American viewpoint. Once I did that, I was made to feel like I was betraying all Indians. I now avoid political discussions with my Indian relatives at all costs.

"All of our foreign service postings have been in Asia, so I have been able to visit India at least once a year. With each visit, I found that I no longer considered Madras home. This was especially true after my mother died."

While we are changing, so are our families. With each visit to Sydney, I found the family gatherings smaller, as grandparents, aunts, and uncles died. Some years ago, my brother was killed in a car accident while on a business trip to Atlanta. He had spent a couple of days with me in Virginia before traveling to Georgia for meetings. The day after I took him to the airport, I received a call from my distraught mother telling me of his death. His employer arranged to have his body flown back to Australia, and my husband and I flew to Sydney for the funeral. Although nobody gave me any reason to feel that way, I remember feeling embarrassed and unreasonably responsible because he had died in "my" country.

Now, the world I revisit when I go back to Sydney is my mother's. My own friends faded from my life years ago, and the people who are invited to tea to see me on my visits are my mother's friends. I have known most of them all my life, but each time, there are fewer of them as well.

Didem has been back to visit her family in Istanbul, Turkey, several times since 1987. "This year when I went back I realized that, although I love my country and so forth, I could not live there," she said. "The place where I grew up is changed, so much has changed...I cried actually. It's a different place for me now, and I am not involved in what's going on there. Also, now that I've lived in the United States and become used to a different way of doing things, it would be frustrating to live in Istanbul again.

"I have maybe two friends left. On this trip, I could not get hold of one of them, and the other one and I don't have the same interests anymore. So I spent all my time with my mom's friends. We had a wonderful time, but I would not choose to live like that. I'm a different person. I have an emptiness of not belonging there, and not really belonging here. I have a good marriage, and now I have my daughter, but inside of me, I'm lost. I don't belong anywhere."

Lourdes recently went back to Peru for the first time in thirty years. She had planned to go on several previous occasions, but terrorism and overall unsafe conditions there prevented her from going. Her mother and brother visited her from time to time in the United States and at her overseas posts, but there were cousins she had not seen since she left after her marriage, and their children whom she had never met. After such a long time away, she and her husband were treated as honored guests.

She said, "I was nervous about going, but it was really time for me to go back. My mother is eighty-six and I had not seen her in five years. After my father died, years ago, she lived for a while with her sister in Spain and I visited her there, but in the early 1990s she moved back to Lima. When the time comes, she wants to be buried there beside my father. I wasn't nervous about meeting the family but I was worried that my memories of the Lima of my childhood would be spoiled. Because of all the problems they have had there I was expecting the city to be run-down, but it wasn't. Everything was so clean. I had a wonderful time.

"The welcome for my husband and me from my family was unbelievable. I could only take a week and a half from work, so there was not much time. But we had breakfasts and lunches and dinners, and so many cousins came. I felt such a tranquility and security there surrounded by people who were my family! Some of them expressed surprise that I had kept my Spanish at a good level, and they were pleased to hear that both my son and daughter speak it well. To hear my nieces calling me *tia* was wonderful.

"My brother drove us to every single place I used to go: my school—the wall had been painted green but that was the only difference; my favorite beach—it was exactly the same as before! To get there, you had to go on a very winding road and it looked exactly the same: the kiosks along the beach and a club, although I was told that it's not as popular as before. But it's still there! There are also lots of new and beautiful shopping areas and I felt like a tourist shopping for gifts. We did other tourist things too: visited the Congress (which I never in my life did before); went to a bullfight; saw the changing of the guard at the government palace in the main piazza, which I had never seen. We also went to the cemetery to visit the mausoleum where my father and my older brother are buried. I took pictures for my son, who has my father's name.

"My husband and I stayed with one of my cousins whose house is larger than my family home, which my mother and brother now share. The family house was new when we moved there when I was young, and I must say it looked smaller to me when I went back. The trees in the garden and the park behind are tall now and the open spaces seemed more overgrown. My mother invited old neighbors to tea to meet us.

"Our time there was quite short and I only managed to meet one of my old friends. We had a wonderful time, and I would like to go back for more visits of a month or so. But I would not want to go back to stay. I could not start all over again. Like all Latin systems, it's too complicated and bureaucratic. Even with my family there, it would be too difficult. We're settled here; I would not want to pack up my house again. Plus, my children are here.

"Usually when I come back from vacation I think, 'Oh, no, I have to go back to work.' But this time when I came back, I felt energized. I have a tremendous amount of energy but in a calm way."

When Hala went back to Lebanon with her husband and daughter a couple of years ago, it was her first visit in twenty-five years. She had a similar experience to Lourdes.

She said, "Before the war broke out in Lebanon, my husband and I used to go to visit my family there every summer. After that, we couldn't go at all and my parents moved permanently to the United States. My daughter had never visited Lebanon. Going back was scary because I didn't know how I would feel or how they would feel. Because Lebanon went through such trauma, it wasn't the Lebanon I left, and it was sad to see the changes. I could never go back there and live now, and yet I loved the fact that everybody else looked like me, sounded like me. Everywhere else I've lived, I was always different. Even in the rest of the Arab world where we have been posted, they could tell I was Lebanese.

"It was so nice to go back to walk the streets I walked as a child and a young adult, to go the university I went to, the house we used to live in. All this family I used to have surrounded and embraced me. It was good for my daughter to see the place I went to school and smell the air and see the mountains. I used to tell her how beautiful it was, but it didn't make any sense to her. Seeing it, she could understand what I was talking about and it was good to share that with her."

Two of the women made the decision to move back to their native countries permanently after their husbands died. Neither of them had children, so they were not constrained by family ties to the United States.

One was Australian-born. She and her foreign service officer husband were living in Manila, the Philippines, when he died of lymphoma in 1992. She said, "We were married in 1965 and served in the Middle East and South East Asia. Over the years between postings, we spent little time in the United States. My husband had two children from his previous marriage, but we had none of our own. When he got sick, we talked about what I would do after he died, and he recommended that I stay on in Manila where I would be surrounded by friends. I did that, continuing to rent the house we had shared there. Then in June 1999, the landlady informed me that she wanted the house back for her son, who was returning to the Philippines from Australia. About the same time, my mother-in-law in the United States died. So I decided to leave Manila and return to Melbourne, where I grew up and where my brother still lives. My father had died two years before and my eighty-year-old mother had moved to a seaside town in New South Wales, but my family would have been hurt if I had decided to live in the United States instead.

"It has been very difficult coming back. I can't talk about my foreign service life with friends from my teenage years. I have met some other people who have lived abroad with the United Nations and that has helped. I have joined several clubs—the American Women's Auxiliary and the Asia Society—and I go to lectures from time to time. I'm taking Chinese brush painting lessons, I play tennis, and I go out sailing with my brother, with whom I am staying temporarily.

"But, it's very boring and provincial here, and I thank God that I married and had the life I had. I was blessed with a good life. Will I last here? Oh, I'll probably just get provincial like everybody else!"

Elisabeth Herz, now in her seventies, is living again in Vienna. She had not planned to go back to stay, just to take the year's sabbatical in 1991 from her work at George Washington University Hospital in Washington. But Vienna worked its magic, and Elisabeth fell in love with the city again. When her sabbatical ended, she requested an extension and then, in 1993, made the decision to stay permanently. She rents an apartment just outside the *Ringstrasse*, within walking distance of the Opera House and not far from *Johannesgasse*, where she went to school before the war. The rooms of her apartment contain books, pictures, and other mementoes of the foreign service life she lived with her late husband. Her daily schedule is full: she teaches at the university and sees psychotherapy patients in her home office.

She said, "I had a hard time deciding if I would return to Vienna because it was so marvelous there at George Washington. I was really established in the United States and there were so few of us working on psychosomatic women's problems in the ob/gyn field. However, there were three major reasons for my decision to come back. First of all, I had been longing for the Alps. When I was a child during the Nazi times, the only place I felt free and safe was in the mountains, where my friends and I could talk without being overheard. The mountains to me mean freedom. Obviously, I experienced freedom in the United States, but these mountains have a special emotional pull. The second reason was that the Iron Curtain was down and there seemed now to be a chance for a united Europe and I wanted to be in Austria to experience this. Through Alpbach and the few friends who are still alive and active there, I am right in the middle of all these things. The third reason was that I wanted to bring back all the medical knowledge I had acquired during my years away. The decision was still really hard, but when I did finally decide, somehow it felt right. It was a feeling of the circle closing."

It was not all easy. She was a different person from the young woman who had left in 1957. Her colleagues at the university did not welcome her with open arms. If her opinions differed from those of her friends in a discussion about the United States, her friends would say, "Oh, well, but you're American." She censored herself in conversations at first, but on one point she acknowledges they are right:

"I had without noticing it myself taken on a number of the typical characteristics of Americans, things that I don't want to lose. People here in Austria when faced with something they don't like will say, 'Well, you can't do anything about it anyway.' Whereas in the United States, it's just the opposite: 'OK, there is a problem. What can we do about it?' I really feel like a product of both cultures.

"The other thing which I found, and to a certain extent do still find difficult, is that when I am in a large social gathering and people are talking about events or people who are household names, I have no idea who they are because I have been away practically forty years. So when I ask: 'Well, who is that?' they look at me as if I have early Alzheimer's syndrome."

Although there is a gap in her Austrian experience that separates her from her friends and colleagues, she does share the experience of the Nazi times, and the friends who remain from those years are the closest. She said, "I realize that it is important for me here to have a few friends who have also lived in the United States or at least abroad. I have the greatest problems with those who have always stayed here and consider this to be the center of the world. Those who, for example, find that the way one uses knives and forks here is the only educated way to use them and what a terribly misbehaved person you are if you do not know how it is done!

When you have lived in so many different cultures, you find this just ridiculous.

"So for different reasons, I do not feel any more that I belong here in the same way as I belonged before. I also don't feel I totally belong when I am in the United States. When I am feeling down sometimes, I think, 'Poor me, I don't really belong anywhere anymore.' But, when I am in a good mood, I feel how lucky I am that I have had all these opportunities to live in other countries and to experience them through my work. I had very special experiences, which definitely made me richer and widened my horizons. I am cosmopolitan, and I thank God it is this way."

Most of the women have gone through stages of separation from their former countries. The young ones try in the beginning to maintain their connections and are hopeful they can pass the attachment to place and family along to their children. Cheaper ways of communication today help maintain personal connections: e-mail has made an enormous difference in exchanging up-to-the-minute family news. When I left Australia, telephone charges were so expensive that we called only in times of emergency or at Christmas, when we had to book ahead to make a call at a specific time. Now I can talk for an hour for a few dollars. Airfares are certainly cheaper today than in past years. It is also possible to read a hometown newspaper on the Internet and watch local television by satellite.

On my latest trip to Sydney in March of 2000, I spent a morning in the city. It was a beautiful warm day, and I found a seat on a bench along Circular Quay. The tiled roof of the Opera House gleamed white against the deep blue, cloudless sky. I sat for a while watching the cross-harbor ferries chug back and forth from the piers, leaving seagulls squawking in their wakes. It was a place I had often visited on my lunch hour before I left Sydney in 1966, a short walk from the publisher's office where I worked on George Street. The old building is gone now, replaced by a fancy new high-rise hotel. I used to lean on the railing overlooking the water, throw scraps from my sandwich to the birds, and dream of sailing away on one of the liners that berthed at the overseas terminal.

There was a ship in port that day and groups of tourists strolled along the walkway: French, German, and Japanese. Musicians were playing for the passersby, and I became aware of two competing sounds. From my right came the sound of a bagpipe. A memory stirred: Anzac Day, sprigs of rosemary, a bus ride with my father to a dawn service of remembrance. From my left came a haunting, quivering melody. I turned and saw a young woman with Asian features and dress sitting in the shade of a small tree and playing a stringed instrument that was unfamiliar to me.

The competing sounds symbolized for me the changes that had occurred in Australia. The old Australia in which I grew up no longer exists; the new one is a place in which I am almost as much a tourist as the Germans and French and Japanese who were taking photographs of the harbor in front of me. It was actually comforting to contemplate the new, and I felt relieved of some of my guilt feelings. It was not only I who had changed. While I love my family and am grateful for my childhood in Australia, I must accept the fact that it is no longer my place.

At the end of my visit, I flew back to the United States. When the immigration official in San Francisco handed me back my passport, he said, "Welcome home." It gave me a good feeling, one that lasted until the first well-meaning person said to me: "Oh, I love your accent. Where are you from?"

Biographical Information

(in alphabetical order, by first name)

Allison (Trinidad and Tobago)

Allison is in her thirties and was married in 1995. She was an elementary school teacher when she met her husband, who was assigned to the American embassy in Port of Spain, Trinidad. Allison's father had met him first at the marathon runners' club they both belonged to, and introduced him to his daughter. The couple has been assigned to Caracas, Venezuela, and Washington, D.C. Allison works for the Department of State.

Anna (New Zealand)

Anna is in her fifties and was married in New Zealand in 1980. She was raised in Christchurch and, after university, worked for the New Zealand Treasury Department for a year, then left for the United Kingdom on a "working holiday." She took a year to get there, working for some of the time as a local hire in the New Zealand embassy in Bangkok, Thailand. Four years later, she returned to New Zealand and joined the diplomatic service as an administrative/consular officer. After three months in Wellington, she was posted to San Francisco for three and a half years and then to Athens, Greece, where she met her husband, who was assigned to the American embassy there. They also have been posted to Papua New Guinea, Turkey, Australia, New Zealand, and the United Kingdom. They have two sons.

Annabella (Guatemala)

Annabella is in her thirties and was married in 1983. The eldest of three girls, she was educated in a Catholic girls' school. After school, she went to work as a secretary for the U.S. Agency for International Development (AID) in Guatemala where she met her husband. They have two children and have been posted to El Salvador, Belize, Ecuador, and Romania.

Anna Maria (Italy)

Anna Maria is in her fifties. She met her husband in the American consulate in Rome, where she had gone to get a visa to the United States to visit her sister. She recalled, "I had left it till the last minute and was in a panic. I parked my motorcycle on the curb and went in for my interview. I didn't speak any English and dealt with a local employee. His American supervisor came over to verify some of my answers (he spoke very little Italian) and was then called away to the phone. I thought the interview was over so I picked up my passport, which was already stamped and under the glass that separates the applicant from the interviewer, and left. When I got back to work (I was working in a boutique with a friend of mine), the phone rang and it was the American supervisor saying that there were some questions I had not answered and could he also invite me out for lunch to make some suggestions about what I should see in the States. So we had lunch. When I was unpacking after I returned from my trip, I received a note that was pushed under my door. (I didn't have a telephone.) His Italian had improved during the weeks that I had been away. We started going out." They were married in 1978 and had two tours in Guatemala and one in Brazil. Anna Maria's husband died in 1997.

Bibi (India)

Now in her fifties, Bibi was married at nineteen to her first cousin in 1962. Her father was an Indian diplomat and she was raised outside India. She has worked as an art teacher in the United States and overseas. She has accompanied her husband on assignments to India, Mexico, and South Korea. They have a son and a daughter.

Bo-Yeon (South Korea)

Born in Seoul in 1955, Bo-Yeon has two brothers and three sisters. She waged a long and painful campaign for her father's permission to leave home in 1977 to work as a flight attendant for Cathay Pacific Airways, based in Hong Kong. In her last year of college, she quietly collected all the paperwork, and told her parents about it only when she had passed all the interviews and received her passport. Worn down by her determination, her father finally relented.

In 1979, she was introduced by a friend to an American who was working at the U.S. consulate in Hong Kong. He came from a very small town in Colorado and, at thirty-three, seemed a confirmed bachelor. Within months, however, they decided to get married, and Bo-Yeon flew to Seoul to tell her family. Her father's reaction to her intention to marry a non-Korean was silence—a month-long silence—but eventually he agreed to meet her fiancé. He told Bo-Yeon to bring him to Seoul, with an interpreter. The couple made six trips between Hong Kong and Seoul before Bo-Yeon's father agreed to the marriage. (Years later, she learned that during this period, her father hired an investigator to look into her fiancé's background.)

Bo-Yeon has accompanied her husband to posts in Indonesia, the Philippines, Austria, and Germany. They have a son and a daughter.

Carmen (Chile)

Carmen is in her thirties and was married in 1997. She met her husband in Santiago, where she was working and where he was assigned to the American embassy. After their marriage, they moved to Washington, D.C. Unable to speak English when she arrived in the United States, Carmen is now studying for a master of business administration degree at American University.

Chris (England)

Chris was born in 1939 in Liverpool. She went to an all-girls' school and then to Liverpool University, where she studied history. Later, she completed a graduate secretarial course and earned a certificate of education.

She worked in a government office in London and then moved back to Liverpool to teach. She met her husband there while he was visiting a friend. He was at that time a lawyer teaching in Liberia and waiting to be accepted into AID. They were married and moved to New York and then Washington, D.C., in 1968. Their overseas postings have been to Pakistan, Haiti, Ghana, Egypt, and Bulgaria. They have a son and a daughter.

Dany (Germany)

Dany is in her thirties and was married in 1994. She met her husband in Mongolia, where she had gone to teach English and where he was serving with the Peace Corps. They moved to the Solomon Islands with the Peace Corps after their marriage in Germany and have since been posted with the foreign service to Uzbekistan and China.

Didem (Turkey)

Now in her thirties, Didem married at twenty in Istanbul in 1984. The middle child of three children, she attended a technical high school and then went to work as a private secretary. She met her husband, who was assigned to the American consulate as a communicator, at a wedding in Istanbul. They have been posted to Liberia and Somalia and have one daughter.

Elisabeth Herz (Austria)

Elisabeth Herz is a gynecologist/obstetrician and a psychiatrist. Born in 1926, she grew up in Vienna, where she did her medical training. After her marriage to FSO Martin Herz in 1957, she moved with him to Japan, and subsequently to Iran, South Vietnam, and Bulgaria. She practiced medicine as a volunteer in Tokyo, Tehran, and Saigon. In Washington, D.C., she practiced as an ob/gyn at George Washington University Medical Clinic and the Group Health Association and served as a consultant to the

Columbia Hospital for Women. She completed a residency in psychiatry at George Washington University Medical Center, and her last position in Washington was director of the Center's psychosomatic program in ob/gyn.

Widowed since 1983, Elisabeth now lives in Vienna, where she teaches at the University of Vienna and is a practicing psychotherapist specializing in psychosomatic obstetrics and gynecology, including research into post-partum depression.

Faye Barnes (Canada)

Faye is in her fifties and was married in 1968. She comes from a small community in Saskatchewan, a hundred miles north of the North Dakota/Montana border. She met her husband in graduate school at the University of Minnesota where she received a master of arts in food science. She subsequently worked for General Mills. Her husband joined the Foreign Agricultural Service in 1970. They have two daughters and have served in Venezuela, Spain, Peru, Germany, Mexico, and the United Kingdom.

Frederique (France)

Frederique is in her thirties. She met her husband in the early 1990s in Germany, where she was teaching French at a language institute and where he was a student. Her hometown is in the Alps, and she has worked as a ski instructor as well as an interpreter/translator. She has a master of arts in applied foreign languages and she majored in English and German. She and her husband have been posted to Tblisi, Georgia. They have one son.

Hala (Lebanon)

Now in her fifties, Hala met and married her husband in Beirut in 1968. She had just come back from a year studying interior design in New

York and was working for the cultural affairs officer at the U.S. Information Service (USIS) saving the money to go back to finish her degree. He was studying Arabic at the Foreign Service Institute in Beirut. After their marriage, they moved to South Yemen and have since been posted to Mauritania, Kuwait, Oman, Iraq, Canada, and Saudi Arabia. Hala works as an art therapist. They have one daughter.

Helga (Germany)

Helga is in her forties. She is one of three children of a German diplomat and grew up moving from country to country. She returned to Germany for university and studied law. She speaks German, English, Spanish, and French. She met her husband in 1984 in Germany, where he was assigned to the American embassy. They also have been posted to Russia and Holland. They have two sons.

Inger (Denmark)

Inger was born in 1949 in Copenhagen. Her father was the headmaster of a boarding school. When she was fifteen she came to the United States as an exchange student and spent a year in Massachusetts. In 1969, as a student nurse at the biggest hospital in Copenhagen and the only person on the ward at the time who spoke English, she was asked to take care of an American diplomat who had been very badly injured in an automobile accident. They were married in 1971, stayed on in Denmark for a year, and then moved to Washington, D.C. They have been posted to Madagascar, Malawi, the Philippines, Switzerland, and Sri Lanka (with the Colombo Plan). They have a son and a daughter.

In Soon (South Korea)

In Soon is in her fifties. She was born in Kwangju. Her mother's family lived in Japan and her father also studied and worked there. One of seven children, In Soon was raised by her grandparents in Kwangju. After high school, she went to college in Seoul, where she graduated with a degree in journalism. She worked as a producer with a radio station and then moved to Tegu where she was a reporter for the same station. She met her husband at a seminar at the U.S. Information Service (USIS) office in Tegu where he worked. They were married in 1973. They have a daughter and a son and have been assigned to Japan, South Korea (twice), and Sri Lanka.

Jennie (Taiwan)

Jennie is in her thirties. She came to the United States to study in 1988 and met her husband in New York the following year. They married in 1995 and have been posted to Beijing, China. They have one daughter.

Latha (India)

Latha is in her forties. She comes from Madras and was educated in a Catholic school there. She was working as a secretary at the U.S. Information Service (USIS) when she met her husband, a USIS officer. They married in the United States in 1978 and have two daughters. They also have been posted to Nepal and Sri Lanka.

Lesley Dorman (England)

Lesley's father was an American businessman; her mother was British. Born in England and raised with her younger sister at the family's country home, Lesley was sent away to boarding school when she was ten. She had just finished school when World War II broke out, and she joined the British Army. After the war, she lived in London, where she met her husband. He was on his second posting (after Moscow) at the American embassy. They were married in 1950 and stayed on in London, until his assignment was up in 1953 and he was posted to Cairo, Egypt. Now in her seventies, Lesley is a longtime volunteer and office-holder in the Associates of the American Foreign Service Worldwide (AAFSW). She was one of the leaders of the campaign to establish the Family Liaison Office (FLO) at the Department of State. An account of this effort can be found in *Married to the Foreign Service* by Jewell Fenzi. As well as in Egypt, Lesley has served with her husband in Iran, Northern Rhodesia/Zambia, Sudan, and Thailand. They have two sons.

Lois (Wales)

Now in her forties, Lois grew up between Cardiff and Swansea in the south of Wales. She moved with her first husband to Lesotho. After they divorced, Lois stayed on and worked there for seven years. She met her American husband while he was assigned to the American embassy there and after their marriage, in 1984, moved to Bonn, Germany. They also have been posted to Cuba, Mexico, Thailand, and a second tour in Germany (Frankfurt). They have two sons.

Lourdes (Peru)

One of three children and the only daughter, Lourdes was educated at the British school in Lima and at college in the United States. She met her husband in Lima, where he was assigned to the American embassy. Married in 1971, she is now in her fifties and has a daughter and a son. She has been assigned to Spain, Argentina, and Austria.

Maggy (Belgium)

Maggy met her husband in 1962 in Brussels, where she was born and raised. After college she worked as a translator—French is her mother tongue and she also speaks English, German, and Dutch. She later worked for Sabena Belgian World Airlines in a program to provide language services at Brussels airport, and also as a flight attendant. She is now in her fifties and works for the Department of State. She and her husband have two sons. The family's postings have been to Indonesia, Malaysia, Kuwait, Italy, Belgium, Sweden, Israel, and Haiti.

Maria Bauer (Czechoslovakia, now the Czech Republic)

Maria grew up in Prague, one of three daughters of a wealthy business-man. She was educated at home until she was twelve years old and then was sent to the French Lycée in Prague. While at university, she was introduced to Robert Bauer, a Viennese-born lawyer who had left Austria when the Germans invaded. He was working as a reporter for the *New York Times* in Prague, and Maria met him at social functions from time to time. When the German invasion of Czechoslovakia was imminent, Maria and her parents managed to flee to France. Robert also made his way to Paris, where he and Maria were reunited. From there, he engineered the family's escape to Portugal. Maria and Robert were married in Caldas in Portugal in 1940 before they and Maria's parents managed to secure visas to the United States. The four of them traveled to New York by steamer. Their first home was an apartment on the West Side. Maria was twenty-one years old and her husband ten years older. [It is a long and complicated story and I rec-ommend reading all of it in Maria's memoir, *Beyond the Chestnut Trees.*] After some time, Robert found work with Voice of America in New York and eventually the family transferred to Washington, D.C., where he went to work for USIS. They have been assigned overseas to Iran, India, and Egypt. They have a son and a daughter.

Michele (France)

Michele calls herself a *pied noir*, born in Morocco but a product of French culture. Her mother was born Italian and naturalized French at age seven. Her father is a Parisian. Her parents moved from Morocco to West Africa in 1950, when Michele was ten, living first in Guinea, and then settling in

Bamako in what was then French Sudan, and today is Mali. She studied by correspondence under the supervision of her father and worked for him for three years as a clerk/secretary.

She met her husband in 1961 (she was twenty-one), when he was on his first foreign service tour in Bamako. "He lived across the road from us and we had the only tennis court in the country in our yard," she said. "He could not resist!" They were married a few months before he was due to be transferred to Lebanon. They have since been posted to South Yemen, Libya, Jordan (twice), and Saudi Arabia. They have a son and a daughter.

Muriel (Belgium)

Muriel, now in her fifties, comes from Brussels. She met her husband in Guinea, West Africa, in 1971. She said, "I had traveled within Europe quite a bit but not outside, and I decided to move somewhere else to see a bit more of the world. A headhunter friend said, 'How about Conakry?' I said, 'Tell me more.' 'Guinea, West Africa.' 'Is it on the sea?' Yes. 'OK, I'll take it.' I got the job. It was with a Belgian company tracking appropriated funds for bauxite. Conakry was a hardship post, but I never regretted going there. The expatriate community was very friendly and we socialized and supported each other a lot. The second year I was there, I met my future husband, who was on his first posting at the American embassy." They were married in the United States in 1973 and have a son and a daughter. They have been posted to Algeria, India, Central African Republic, Mauritius, and Austria.

Rekha (India)

Rekha's father was in the Indian Navy and she grew up in Madras. She attended a small women's college in Virginia and returned to Madras after graduation. She was doing public relations work for the Sheraton hotel when a mutual acquaintance introduced her to her future husband, who was assigned to the American consulate in Madras. Now in her forties, Rekha is an American foreign service officer, "proud to represent a country that welcomes foreign-borns into its diplomatic corps." She and her husband have served in Nepal, Pakistan, and Thailand. They have two daughters.

Salote (Fiji)

Salote was twenty-nine and a bank manager in Suva when she met her husband there in 1985. She is the eighth of ten children and her father was a repairman with the Royal New Zealand Air Force. When she and her husband met, he was thirty-eight and on the Peace Corps staff, having previously served as a volunteer in Fiji and the Solomon Islands. After he left the Peace Corps, he joined the foreign service and his first post was Lagos, Nigeria. Subsequent postings have been to Sri Lanka and Fiji. They have a son and a daughter.

Sangeeta (Japan)

Sangeeta, now in her thirties, was born in Osaka and grew up in Kobe. Her mother is Japanese; her father was Indian. She traveled to the United States to attend Georgetown University, graduating in 1983. She met her husband at Georgetown and they were married in Japan in 1985. They have been assigned to the Philippines, Japan, Taiwan, and China.

Susi (Kuwait)

Susi's father was Kuwaiti and her mother is German. She was raised in Kuwait with a strong European influence, spending summers in Germany with her mother's family, and speaking both German and Arabic. Susi did her undergraduate work, in economics and European social and economic history, at Bristol University in England. After graduation, she returned to Kuwait and worked at the Kuwait National Museum for three years. When the Iraqis invaded Kuwait, her family was out of the country on holiday and she was on her own. A few months into the occupation, she managed to get out and travel to London. She already had her application in at the London School of Oriental Studies for postgraduate work, so she carried on with her plans to study Islamic art and archaeology there. She returned to Kuwait after that, but the museum had been destroyed during the war so she could not get her old job back. Instead, she took a position as senior economic officer at the British embassy.

She met her husband in 1992 in Kuwait, where he was working at the American embassy. Certain that her father would never give her permission to marry a foreigner and leave, she told him she wanted to go to New York to study for a doctorate. When he heard that she had married in the United States, he told all of her friends that she was dead. They were not reconciled until just before he died. Now in her thirties, Susi has accompanied her husband on assignment to Switzerland. They have one daughter.

Tanja (Croatia)

Tanja, now in her thirties, was born and raised in Vukovar, a Croatian town that used to hold about 40,000 people but is now mostly rubble. During her high school years, Tanja spent some time in England and now she speaks fluent English. She moved to Zagreb in 1982 to attend medical school and stayed on after graduation. Her father, who is Serbian, and her mother, who is Croatian, separated during the war and are now divorced. Her mother moved to Zagreb in 1991, as a displaced person, and her father stayed in Vukovar.

Tanja met her husband in Zagreb where she was working for the United Nations High Commission for Refugees (UNHCR) and he was working at the American embassy, dividing his time between consular and political work. He worked closely with the United Nations on refugee programs. They were married in 1995 and have been assigned to the American embassy in Zaire (Congo) and with the United Nations in Croatia. They have two daughters.

Wati (Indonesia)

Wati, now in her fifties, was thirty-one when her future American husband proposed. He was eight years older than she, working for AID in Jakarta. Her parents waived the normal engagement preliminaries but did request a formal letter from his parents stating their support for the marriage. It was delivered, and translated into Indonesian. Wati's parents were happy about the match: their future son-in-law had lived in Indonesia for seven years and had a good understanding of their culture. They were satisfied that he would treat their daughter with respect.

"I come from what I would call the hard-core of Javanese, from Java Island," Wati said. "My hometown is Yogyakarta, an historical town. I am the tenth of twelve children, the only one who has left Indonesia. The majority of the population is Muslim, but our family is Catholic, the same as my husband's. I was interested in foreign languages, and English was the one I thought I could learn. So after high school, I went to live with my elder sister in Solo, about two hours to the east of Yogyakarta and studied at a two-year teacher's college to prepare as an English teacher at the middle school level. When I finished, I decided I would rather work for an international organization. This meant more study so I moved back to my hometown and enrolled myself at the teacher's institute and earned a bachelor's degree in English.

"After graduation I moved to Jakarta, where another sister was living, and found a job as a receptionist at a five-star hotel, using my English. I then worked as a secretary for a consultant with American Population Control under the Indonesian National Family Planning Board. When his contract was up two years later, I applied for a job at the American embassy in the USIS educational exchanges office. After two years there, I moved over to AID where I was hired on the basis of my national family planning background. My husband was working for AID and that's how we met."

They were married in 1981 and have since been posted to Fiji, Papua New Guinea, and Sri Lanka. They have a son and a daughter.

Notes

Note to the Reader

1. USIA/USIS was an independent government agency until 1999, when it was absorbed by the Department of State.

Chapter One

1. FSI—the Foreign Service Institute, the National Foreign Affairs Training Center, located in Arlington, Virginia, where FSOs attend training courses and language classes.

2. According to Ann Miller Morin in her book *Her Excellency: An Oral History of American Women Ambassadors*, female foreign service officers resigned not because there was an official directive on the subject, but because it was the custom. The practice was stopped in the 1970s and some women were readmitted (p.10). However, a regulation did exist that foreign service officers had to be available for worldwide service (3FAM629). Perhaps it was presumed that because they were married, the women could not satisfy this requirement.

3. See State Department manual (3FAM629).

4. Before World War II, Elisabeth's father worked for the Austrian Department of the Interior, which included the police force. He was in charge of identifying and removing Nazi infiltrators from the police training academy. When the Germans took over Austria, he was arrested and put on trial. He was released but fired from his job and not permitted to take another. The private girls' school that Elisabeth attended before the war was closed down and she was moved to a public school, which was run by a Nazi administration.

To counteract the Nazi propaganda that was being fed to the children, some Catholic priests started to meet with groups of them in secret. Elisabeth was a member of one of these secret groups. Because of her father's former position, the family's anti-Nazi sentiments were known. Elisabeth and two of her friends were alerted by another classmate that they were going to be called for an interview about the meetings. This enabled the girls to agree on a consistent story and they survived the questioning. One of the priests was subsequently arrested, however, and sent to a concentration camp. The groups were disbanded.

5. Elmore F. Rigamer, M.D., *Diplomacy: The Role of the Wife,* ed. Martin F. Herz, 53, 54.

Chapter Two

1. A-100 class. Seven-week orientation class for new foreign service officers held at the Foreign Service Institute, Arlington, Virginia. "The orientation program focuses on the operation of the Department of State, the foreign affairs community, and the life of a diplomat abroad. The program consists of lectures, discussions, writing and speaking exercises, and visits to other government agencies." Source: U.S. Department of State web site.

2. OBC. Overseas Briefing Center, located at the National Foreign Affairs Training Center in Arlington, Virginia. A resource center for FSOs and their families.

3. Jenel Virden, *Good-bye Piccadilly: British War Brides in America,* 121.

4. Each fall, the Overseas Briefing Center presents two workshops aimed at foreign-born spouses: one on cross-cultural marriage and one on transition to life in Washington, D.C.

5. Citizenship requirement for foreign-born spouses: State Department manual (3FAM629). June 18, 1987, is the official date that the requirement for citizenship was dropped. Source: Directives

Management Staff via the Office of the Historian, Department of State.

6. U.S. Department of State web site: "Although the Family Liaison Office provides assistance to all foreign affairs agencies in other program areas, FLO's naturalization assistance is limited to Department of State spouses due to the large number of new and pending cases. FLO will provide general guidance to spouses from other agencies and work with office counterparts to share information."

Chapter Three

1. Virden, *Good-bye Piccadilly*, 35, 39, 41, 113. British war brides were accused of being "fast and loose," "gold-diggers," and women "who had fooled around and hooked an American to better [their] standard of living through free immigration to the United States."

Chapter Four

1. Forum of the AAFSW, *The Role of the Spouse in the Foreign Service*, vii.

2. U.S. Department of State web site.

3. "Study: Family Needs $50,000 for Basics," *Washington Post*, 17 November 2000, Metro section. A study by Wider Opportunities for Women, a D.C.-based nonprofit group, for Montgomery County, Maryland, social services, published November 2000.

4. Family Liaison Office, *Direct Communication Project: Bilateral Work Agreements* (Washington, D.C.: U.S. Department of State, February 2000). There are bilateral agreements with eighty-two countries and de facto agreements with fifty-four countries.

5. Family Liaison Office, *Employment Options for Foreign Service Family Members* (Washington, D.C.: U.S. Department of State, January 2001).

6. Language levels at FSI are graded between 1 and 4, with 4 being the highest.

Chapter Five

1. Dr. Ruth Hill Useem pioneered research in the 1950s on children she named Third Culture Kids.
2. Strine is a name given to Australian vernacular. If you say "Australian" very quickly, you will hear "Strine."

Chapter Six

1. "Senior wives" refers to those women who are married to ambassadors, deputy chiefs of mission, and officers who are embassy section heads, such as the political counselor.
2. The "square footage rule" decreed that the area of a house at post should not exceed the number of square feet a family in the Washington, D.C., Metropolitan Area would typically occupy. (Ref. 6FAM721.1)
3. AAFSW/Secretary of State's Award for Outstanding Volunteerism is given to a number of individuals each year for volunteer activities overseas. Winners have been employees as well as family members.
4. Martin Herz wrote a book about his experiences: *215 Days in the Life of an American Ambassador (Diary Notes from Sofia, Bulgaria)*. (Washington, D.C.: School of Foreign Service, Georgetown University, 1981).

Chapter Eight

1. Jewell Fenzi, *Married to the Foreign Service*, 212–214.
2. Family Liaison Office, *The Foreign Service Family & Divorce* (Washington, D.C.: U.S. Department of State, 2000), 1.
3. Ibid., 13.

Chapter Nine

1. Dugan Romano, *Intercultural Marriage*, Chapter 1.
2. Family Liaison Office, *Direct Communication Project: Elder Care in the Foreign Service* (Washington, D.C.: U.S. Department of State, 2000), 9–10.
3. See State Department manual (3FAM3740) for Emergency Visitation Travel rules implemented January 16, 2001.

Chapter Ten

1. Maria Bauer, *Under the Chestnut Trees*.
2. When Carol Laise was ambassador to Nepal in the late 1960s, Ellsworth Bunker was ambassador to South Vietnam. Martin Herz was political counselor under Ambassador Bunker. In Carol Laise's absence, Elisabeth Herz sometimes served as hostess at the ambassador's residence. President Johnson had put an airplane at Ambassador Bunker's disposal so that he could travel to Katmandu to visit his wife, and Elisabeth rode along on some of the trips.

Glossary

AAFSW	Associates of the American Foreign Service Worldwide (formerly known as the Association of American Foreign Service Women)
Chargé d'affaires	Person placed in charge in the absence of the ambassador
CLO	Community Liaison Office Coordinator
Cone	The term for a particular career path in the foreign service: political cone, consular cone, administration cone
DCM	Deputy Chief of Mission
DOD	Department of Defense
FLO	Family Liaison Office
FSI	Foreign Service Institute
FSN	Foreign Service National—locally hired host country employee
NFATC	National Foreign Affairs Training Center
OBC	Overseas Briefing Center—resource center, provides information and training to FSOs and their families

PO	Principal Officer—senior officer at posts where there is neither an ambassador nor a consul-general
TDY	Temporary Duty (TDYer: someone on temporary duty)
UNHCR	United Nations High Commissioner for Refugees
USAID	United States Agency for International Development
USIA/USIS	United States Information Agency/Service

Bibliography

Foreign Service Life:

Bell, Linda. *Hidden Immigrants: Legacies of Growing up Abroad.* South Bend, Ind.: Notre Dame: Cross Cultural Publications, 1997.
> Interviews with thirteen American adults who grew up overseas, evaluating the impact the experience had on their adult lives.

Fenzi, Jewell. *Married to the Foreign Service: An Oral History of the American Diplomatic Spouse.* New York: Twayne, 1994.
> Oral histories of American women married to foreign service officers. Provides a history of their bureaucratic struggles with the State Department as well as their personal experiences.

The Forum of the Association of American Foreign Service Women. *Report on the Role of the Spouse in the Foreign Service.* Washington, D.C.: AAFSW, 1985.
> A research study of spouses in five foreign affairs agencies.

Herz, Martin F., ed. *Diplomacy: The Role of the Wife.* Washington, D.C.: Institute for the Study of Diplomacy, Georgetown University, 1981.
> Case studies and commentaries included in a symposium on the U.S. and foreign diplomatic community.

Hickman, Katie. *Daughters of Britannia: The Lives & Times of Diplomatic Wives.* London: HarperCollins, 1999.
> Based for the most part on letters and journals, a history of wives in the British foreign service.

Hughes, Katherine L. *The Accidental Diplomat: Dilemmas of the Trailing Spouse.* New York: Aletheia Publications, 1999.
> A thesis based on interviews with American foreign service spouses, mostly on their dissatisfaction with the life.

Kiyonaga, Bina Cady. *My Spy: Memoir of a CIA Wife.* New York: Avon Books, 2000.
> Sheds light on the wife's role in the career of a CIA officer.

Lord, Bette Bao. *Legacies: A Chinese Mosaic.* New York: Alfred A. Knopf, 1990.
> As the wife of the American ambassador in Beijing, Chinese-born Bette Bao Lord collected stories from individual Chinese. A unique example of the access a foreign-born diplomatic spouse has in the culture from which she comes.

McCluskey, Karen Curnow, ed. *Notes from a Traveling Childhood.* Washington, D.C.: Foreign Service Youth Foundation, 1994.
> First-person accounts by foreign service children.

Related books:

Bauer, Maria. *Beyond the Chestnut Trees.* New York: The Overlook Press, 1984.
> A memoir of a Czech woman who escaped from Prague at the beginning of World War II with her parents and the man who would become her husband. Years later, her husband worked for Voice of America and the United States Information Agency and she traveled with him to posts in Iran, India, and Egypt.

Blackman, Ann. *Seasons of Her Life.* New York: Scribner, 1998.
> A biography of Madeleine Albright.

Brooks, Geraldine. *Nine Parts of Desire: The Hidden World of Islamic Women*. New York: Anchor Books, Doubleday, 1995.
> Contains an account of the role played by American-born Queen Noor in Jordanian-American relations during the Gulf War, and how she was viewed by Jordanians.

Cooke, Hope. *Time Change*. New York: Simon & Schuster, 1980.
> The autobiography of Hope Cooke, the American woman who married the king of Sikkim in the 1970s.

Danquah, Meri Nana-Ama, ed. *Becoming American: Personal Essays by First Generation Immigrant Women*. New York: Hyperion, 2000.
> Essays written by women who either grew up in the United States as children of immigrants, or who came to the country as adults.

Desai, Anita. *Clear Light of Day*. New York: Harper & Row, 1980.
> A novel that paints a telling picture of a foreign service family (in this case Indian) coming home on leave, their reactions to "home" and the impact they have on the family members who stay behind.

Michael, Princess of Kent. *Crowned in a Far Country: Portraits of Eight Royal Brides*. New York: Weidenfeld & Nicolson, 1986.
> Stories of eight princesses married off to become queens of foreign countries.

Romano, Dugan. *Intercultural Marriage: Promises & Pitfalls*. Yarmouth, Mass.: Intercultural Press, 1997.
> Advice for anyone in or contemplating a cross-cultural marriage.

Terasaki, Gwen. *Bridge to the Sun*. Chapel Hill, N.C.: The University of North Carolina Press, 1957.

A memoir of an American woman who married a Japanese diplomat posted to Washington, D.C., on the eve of World War II. She returned to Japan with him and spent the war years there.

Virden, Jenel. *Good-bye Piccadilly: British War Brides in America*. Urbana and Chicago: University of Illinois Press, 1996.
Based on responses to a questionnaire and other research, this fascinating book follows British war brides from the war years through to the present day.

Zweig, Stefan. *Marie Antoinette*. New York: Garden City Publishing Company, 1933.
An acclaimed biography by a famous Austrian writer about Marie Antoinette, a very unfortunate foreign-born spouse.

Index

0-595-22521-7